THE GLOVES COME OFF

By Lisa Petrocelli

Aventine Press

"In her new book, The Gloves Come Off, Lisa Petrocelli takes readers behind the secretive curtain of the biker lifestyle to discover that the American biker is much more than the bad boy image portrayed in films, on TV and in books and newspaper articles. The book offers fifteen road-worthy biographies showing a true cross-section of the motorcycle riding population, from the hardcore Leatherneck, the original Boozefighter, and the one-percenter patch holder, to the biker as caring father, loving husband, and true brother. As one lifelong biker tells us, "Its not just what I do, it's who I am." Many books have tried to give readers an idea of what it is like to live, eat and breathe motorcycles, but The Gloves Come Off really delivers. These bikerographies come straight from the heart and that heart beats to the thunderous rhythm of a Harley-Davidson."

---Dave Nichols, Editor Easyriders & V-Twin Magazine, Paisano Publications, LLC

"A good writer doesn't just go out and do research on the biker world or start right out asking a bunch of questions. No. It doesn't work like that. Not here. You need to talk to people; get to know them. Show respect. Lisa Petrocelli has done just that in The Gloves Come Off. It's a great and intimate portrait of the best lifestyle there is!

---Bill Hayes, National Press & Publicity Officer, Boozefighters MC; Author of "The Original Wild Ones," "American Biker," and "The One-Percenter Encyclopedia."

"This is a strong, well-written book about pride, brotherhood, and faith between brothers. It's about men and women who share motorcycles, the vehicle of freedom for so many, yet understood by so few."

---K. Randall Ball, Editor, Bikernet.com & Author of "Terry the Tramp: The Life and Dangerous Times of a One-Percenter"

Cover and glove photography by Dino Petrocelli

Some words, model names, and designations mentioned herein are the property of the trademark holder. We use them for identification and educational purposes only. This is not an official publication.

Published by Aventine Press
55 East Emerson St.
Chula Vista CA, 91911
www.aventinepress.com

ISBN: 1-59330-769-1

Library of Congress Control Number: 2012906933
Library of Congress Cataloging-in-Publication Data
The Gloves Come Off/ Lisa Petrocelli
Printed in the United States of America

Dedicated to my parents, Marie and Louis Padula,
who taught me how to "lift my veil."

~

TABLE OF CONTENTS

* PREFACE *

~

A Different Kind of Sandbox

"It's in your soul that the true distortion lies."
(Phantom of the Opera)

There is another world that exists in our midst, a world of extreme diversity, and virtually unknown to many. Bikers (or motorcyclists) are a most prominent part of our society, yet ignorance and misconceptions pervade which threaten to drive this American subculture to extinction.

My experience has taught me that bikers are indeed a different breed in some aspects, but at the same time in many ways, no different than the rest of the people we pass as we live our daily lives. The reader may not know any of the men in this book, but chances are that one or more of them resemble the bikers in your life. They roar past your house on their motorcycles, they pass you on the street or in the mall as you go about your daily routine. Bikers share more than motorcycles and leather. They share the best years of their lives, together in their own colorful sandbox.

Except for the chapters regarding my perceptions of the biker community around me, which include men and women, the primary focus of this book is on the male biker. Women motorcyclists, whether drivers or passengers, are as much a part of the biker subculture as men and deserve a novel dedicated only to them.

The men in this book were chosen for a reason. Each has stood out among the crowd and gifted me with a lasting impression. All have graced me with their time and energy in the production of this book. I am forever grateful that they have allowed me the opportunity to listen to their tales of the love, laughter and heartache in their lives, and I am thankful for their trust and respect, which I know has helped them to be as candid as possible with me. The beginning of every man's

chapter features a photograph of his gloves. Each man chose
the gloves depicted here with the only requirement being that
they must have been worn while riding. The gloves represent
their personality and the miles they have traveled.

I asked that each man give careful consideration to this
project when answering my questions, and hopefully their spirit
will be reflected to the reader as you journey with me through
the lives of these men and learn more about the biker and his
soul, as the gloves come off.

~

* QUESTIONS *

~

1. Can you tell me what you would consider the defining moments in your life? You can talk about one or however many you want, but please state what that moment was and why and how it affected you.
2. How old were you when you rode on a motorcycle the first time?
3. Is alcohol or drugs a problem in your life? If so, why?
4. What do you do for a living?
5. Are you married? Kids?
6. How would you describe yourself as a father?
7. What scares you?
8. What is your favorite movie of all time?
9. How do you measure your character and how do you judge the people you surround yourself with?
10. Talk about any regrets you have.
11. Tell me something you wish you had done or still want to do.
12. How many times have you been in love?
13. Club members: What drove you to join a club? If still in, what keeps you in? If out, what drove you out?
14. Did you graduate high school? College? If college, what did you study?
15. Have you ever been close to death? Explain as much or as little as you want.
16. Do you believe wisdom comes with age and experience, or from suffering and surviving?
17. Do you believe in God?
18. Are you close to your family?
19. Why do you love to ride? Explain.
20. Words of wisdom or favorite quote?

BAR
* Ambitious *

"When you're in the Marines, you become a friend of death. It removes the fear of dying and leaves the fear of failing your brothers."

Bar is a member of the Leathernecks Motorcycle Club. Bar is part Irish and Scottish. The name "Barr" is from the same area of Scotland as the Clydesdale, his favorite horse to ride other than a Harley. My first encounter with Bar was when he called and invited me to attend a ceremony celebrating the Marine Corps anniversary in November 2010. The event was held at the site of the USS Slater in downtown Albany, New York. I attended with a friend and enjoyed it immensely. This was a new experience for me, even though I have a brother who is a Marine. I had never witnessed a Marine Corps event before and I was honored to be there. Since then, Bar has continued to invite me to events hosted by the Leathernecks Motorcycle Club, although my schedule so far has prevented me from getting to one.

Bar is very active in the motorcycle community, and his presence is noticed at all occasions, from club parties, charity events, and almost every military-related biker event taking place in our tri-city area. During the past year, Bar has founded an Albany chapter of ABATE (American Bikers Aimed Toward Education), in an effort to further the cause of advocating for bikers' rights and any legislative issues related to bikers in New York State. After much persistence, he finally succeeded in forming the Albany chapter and as President, heads chapter meetings on a monthly basis.

~

"The first time I rode a bike was as a passenger in the 3rd grade. The first time I rode on one alone was my Cushman mini-bike when I was in the 8th grade. The first Harley I rode was in September 1988, when I got back from Okinawa, Japan."

Bar has been riding bikes since he was a young boy. Riding his mini-bike and remembering the feeling of freedom stayed with him throughout his school years and finally, after some time spent in the military, he was able to purchase his first Harley at 20 years old. However, he wasn't able to ride it until he returned to the States in 1988 at 22. Bar has owned five bikes (the 883, GSXR, Interceptor, 1987 Softail Custom and 2007 Street Glide) and now rides two bikes: the Softail and the Street Glide. The 2007 has a "Handicapped" plate on it too. His bike is unmistakable as it has "Semper Fi" on the windscreen.

~

"The day I was adopted by my current family and the day I found my biological mother was when I learned what nature vs. nurture were in my life. I had great adoptive parents; I was adopted when I was about four. So I might have known on my own... but they made sure I knew who I was and that there was a mother out there who had given me up. No one in my adoptive family has ever been in the military. My grandfather, two uncles, and a brother were/ are military. Nature was to be liberal and nurture was to be in the military."

A common thread among the many bikers I know is that in some aspects they are loners, having been raised in broken families or within an unconventional family structure. Bar loves his adoptive parents and is grateful for the sacrifices they've made for him. Although he might have yearned for a close relationship with his biological parents, as he matured, he was wise enough to know that the mother who raised him was the one who nurtured him, led him on the paths he followed, and is in large part responsible for the man he's become. Perhaps his parents knew that the Marines would provide a positive foundation for Bar, and open doors for him that would promise opportunities for his future. Whether intentional or not, Bar embraced military life and seemed destined to be a proud Marine.

~

"I retired from the US Marine Corps after 21 years, four months, and 20 days, moved back to Albany, and bought a duplex. I rent out an apartment to supplement my pension and VA Disability check."

The U.S. Department of Veterans Affairs assesses the cumulative damage done to a person's body while serving, not just combat injuries. Bar has a 60% rating for his feet, knees, hypertension and hands. Now retired and living back in Albany, Bar continues to support the Marines and encourages others to become involved with veterans groups, donating time, energy and financial resources to our soldiers serving overseas as well as the needs of the local veterans in his hometown. He is fortunate in that his retirement allows him to support others. One of the most memorable events he's participated in was visiting Schoharie County after the flooding of Hurricane Irene. There were so many people in need who lost everything. Helping them is the true American Spirit.

~

"I was stationed in California from 1988 to 2001 and then 2003-2006, retiring from a base in California in 2007. I was married twice and left both in Southern California. I do regret a lost love....some people say I'd be a great dad, I'm not so sure."

Bar was married twice, however, admits being in love "for real" only once. He regrets losing the one true love and never having children. So often, it seems that children who have been adopted tend to be drawn to the notion of creating their own family, ideally to dispel the feeling of being alone in this world. Fatherhood may still be a possibility for Bar.

~

"I am physically close to my family here in New York,
but distant from them emotionally because of the typical
crap: veteran returned from combat, family says I've
changed... they forget that they've changed too, fearful
of what I might have done in Iraq and afraid of the media
hype of PTSD in vets. Tried to ease their fears, went to the
VA and got tested, no PTSD.
But it's an underlying issue still."

Life as a soldier in Iraq is a harrowing ordeal. Having to witness the horrors of war while struggling to survive amidst the constant threat of injury or death, naturally takes its toll on a human. Even with the support of the American public and the undaunting force of the U.S. Marine Corps, a soldier ultimately must draw on his or her own inner strength and fortitude to carry on. The stress can be almost unbearable, yet Bar managed to triumph over such adversity and still believes that the U.S. will prevail. The families back home can never truly understand how or why a soldier is forever transformed by the lasting effects of combat. Some of those effects are irreversible.

~

"Not much scares me. I've had to face lots of different
dangers as a Marine. I've learned to face my fears and
overcome them. The ultimate fear is of death. I faced
it by asking to go to Iraq and then volunteering to go
train Iraqis away from the safety of the military camps,
the second most dangerous job in Iraq after being EOD
(Explosive Ordnance Disposal) and diffusing bombs."

Bar's long military career defines who he is today and drives many of his actions within the motorcycle community. No wonder he lists "K-Pax" as his favorite movie, since the charter's name is actually his own legal name, Robert Porter. In addition to his work with the Marines, Bar is a staunch supporter of bikers' rights and will persist in the quest for greater involvement among the biker community to join forces and display a more united front against the police and politicians who seem determined to strip motorcyclists of every right to freedom on the road.

~

"If I have a problem I enjoy riding. I seem more aware of myself and what's around me. My dream would be to ride round-trip to Alaska."

"I try not to judge others so I won't be judged too harshly. As far as my own character, I am one..."

Although we don't know each other too well, I consider Bar a friend. He is personable and will not hesitate to introduce himself to a crowd of strangers. Instead of shying away from challenges, he welcomes them, and is ambitious enough to follow through on the projects he undertakes. One example of this is his determination to create the Albany chapter of ABATE, despite a lack of interest among many Albany bikers. His willingness to accept a leadership role is admired by many.

~

"Re wisdom: If you refuse to learn, you'll be just as stupid at 50 as at five. Try to learn from others' suffering and from your joy."

I share Bar's thoughts on wisdom. I believe our greatest lessons are learned from our own suffering and the suffering of others. The insight gleaned from those experiences is invaluable.

~

"Live as if you were to die tomorrow. Learn as if you were to live forever"...Gandhi

BAR

* HOLLISTER AND THE EVOLUTION OF THE AMERICAN BIKER SUBCULTURE *

~

My brother Rocco asked me if I knew about the origins of marble and oil – that marble is derived from fish and oil is derived from dead dinosaurs. Needless to say, I was a bit taken aback but I decided to poll my coworkers the next day, since they would represent a wide cross-section of personalities and generations. Turns out everyone I talked to was just as shocked as I was with this history lesson. So I got my laptop out and did a Google search and discovered that yes indeed, marble is derived from fish scales and there is a theory that oil may have been developed from dinosaur fossils (hence fossil fuels).

Since I was doing so much research about marble and oil, I decided to do some research on bikers, specifically, on the origin or beginning of the biker subculture. First, I must give credit where credit is due. Much of the information included here was taken from a website called the International Journal of Motorcycle Studies (IJMS): http://ijms.nova.edu/index.html With that said, here is what I learned:

Everything I read about the evolution of the biker subculture seemed to lead to the same conclusion, that is, "In the beginning, there was Hollister." We can blame Marlon Brando for the bad-boy image of bikers and their lifestyle in the 1953 movie, "The Wild One," but "The Wild One" was actually inspired by a short story written by Frank Rooney called "Cyclists' Raid," a fictionalized account of that July 4th weekend of purported violence and revelry in Hollister, a farming community in northern California, in 1947. The press labeled the events a "riot," and the biker became both the object of national scorn and the inspiration for millions of Americans to take up the sport of motorcycling.

Several motorcycle clubs that were in attendance during that weekend in Hollister, including the "Pissed Off Bastards" of Bloomington and the "Boozefighters MC," interrupted an American Motorcyclist Association Gypsy Tour race and caused quite a commotion in town. Gypsy Tours were racing events sanctioned by the American Motorcyclist Association (AMA), held at various locations across the United States. A San Francisco Chronicle photographer, Barney Peterson, was at the scene and decided to create a picture worth a thousand words. Following the Hollister rally, Life Magazine ran Mr. Peterson's photo in their July 21 issue, depicting a drunken biker on a Harley-Davidson surrounded by broken beer bottles. The photo was staged and the article exaggerated, the two combining to create the first American image of the outlaw biker. Mainstream America of 1947 just met a new beast.

The article claimed that an estimated 4,000 members of a motorcycle club were responsible for "the outburst of terrorism," however; no motorcycle club is able to boast even half that number in membership. The events at Hollister were not the work of 4,000 but a small percentage of that number (50% AMA members, 50% bikers out for fun, 500 out for trouble), thus, the origin of the term "one percent" was likely another outcome of the negative publicity. The Boozefighters MC dominated other clubs in attendance, made up almost exclusively of WWII vets. There were a few misdemeanor arrests that weekend but nothing to the extent that "Life Magazine" portrayed. It is really amusing to read that 1947 Life Magazine piece – take a few minutes to read it while keeping in mind the year it was written. The myth is far more sensational than the facts and, ironically, Hollister went to great expense in 1997 to host a 50th anniversary biker rally to commemorate the event!

The end of WWII brought many young soldiers, average age 26, returning home to family and friends. These guys had just experienced the worst of humanity – war and all its ugliness did not help to ease the transition back to a peaceful civilian life. Living through the nightmares, they had naturally bonded together during the war, becoming "brothers in arms." Once again home in their own houses and neighborhoods, that brotherhood was lost and many reported feelings of restlessness and general malaise. Riding motorcycles provided a good substitute for the adrenaline rush they had experienced in combat, as well as relief from the effects of post-traumatic stress, which a good number were probably suffering. It makes perfect sense that the vets would flock together at every opportunity and seek another venue which would offer that brotherhood again.

Bikers, and their perceived intimidating strength and power, became an attraction both feared and envied. Not everyone could become a "wild one," but it seemed that, deep down, everyone wanted to. We all feel so "cool" in our leather jackets, don't we? Why is that? It's because the leather jacket alone conveys a certain fierceness. We assume that the wearer of the black leather jacket is no stranger to danger or intimidation (and we like that). The biker's image has changed little since Hollister, despite ten years of The Fonz on "Happy Days" and the emergence of so many "rich urban bikers" over the years. The sight of a tattooed pack of bikers thundering down the interstate can still inspire dread just by appearing in the rearview mirror, yet, at the same time, motorcycles inspire a longing for the open road and life without responsibility.

Motorcycles represent independence. Bikers are a symbol of freedom and nonconformity. Maybe that explains the longevity of the biker lifestyle or maybe it is just cool. Harley-Davidson has spawned an entire biker subculture and style, with its motorcycles providing the roots, and has changed the course of American history. Harley introduced the first V-twin motorcycle in 1909, and although bicycle racing was America's most popular and well-attended sport in the 1920's, Harley-Davidson was the most popular motorcycle producer in the world at that time, with 2,000 dealers in 67 countries. By the mid-1920s the cost of a small Harley or Indian was around $275, a full size or big-twin model was roughly $375, and the price of a Model T Ford was only $545. The Great Depression had a devastating effect on American motorcycle companies and only two survived – Indian and Harley-Davidson.

Now let's talk about clubs, just a little. While "The Wild One" first introduced the mainstream to the outlaw motorcycle club, those known as "one percenters" were unheard of until the mid-1960's. All one percent clubs are outlaw clubs, but not all outlaw clubs are one percent clubs. The original meaning of the term "outlaw," just meant the absence of an AMA charter, and this still holds in motorcycle clubs that do not define themselves as one percenters. Maybe the outlaw biker is a necessary element of society - attractive yet repellant, hero and anti-hero, citizen and outlaw. However, motorcycle clubs are as varied as the people who make up their membership. The Christian Motorcycle Association, for example, is one of very few faith-based groups that are able to go into "hardcore" biker communities and be well-received ('hardcore' in this case meaning 'one-percenter').

There are two guiding principles of motorcycle clubs: freedom and brotherhood. While the heroes in the Western films often bring law and order to a town in chaos, the bikers seek to throw off the shackles that law and order mandate. Motorcycle clubs are held together by the concept of "love and respect." This concept comes right from the trenches of war when love and respect for those fighting beside you meant survival on physical and mental levels. It also means a true brotherhood, in which feelings and emotions become something so much more than just socializing; they become a way of life.

One fact I found very interesting is that although the Outlaws MC may have been around longer, an all-female motorcycle club, the Motormaids, has maintained an AMA club charter for more than 60 years (the AMA granted their charter in 1940). The Outlaws have experienced at least two organizational changes during their reign; however, the Motormaids have maintained the same governing structure since their inception and may well be the oldest established motorcycle club in the world, older even than the world famous Hells Angels MC (formed in 1947).

I have met many bikers during the few years I've been riding with Dino, people from all walks of life – doctors, lawyers, accountants, business owners, teachers, musicians, moms and dads, aunts and uncles, sisters and brothers, grandmas and grandpas. We all ride for different reasons. Some are young and looking for the new and exciting experiences that come with the territory, others are empty-nesters with disposable incomes, looking for fun and relaxation. For those in between it is a stress-reliever, or simply the call of the wild and the wind.

Most bikers are serious about riding and are concerned about safety for self and others. Bikers embrace each other but also enjoy their separateness from the rest. Within the group, they celebrate their individuality; after all, no two bikes are exactly alike. They ride to fit in *and* to stand out. Somewhere between 1947 and today, in some circles, bikers have gone from villain to hero, as they are indeed a charitable bunch. According to one source, bikers annually contribute well over $10 million, and possibly up to $20 million to charitable organizations!

The motorcycle does not discriminate, and that fact alone is what makes the biker subculture so widespread and legendary. There are many riders among the wealthy and even the super wealthy. Among the celebrities who enjoy riding are Jay Leno (was also a mechanic as a young man), Malcolm Forbes, Bob Dylan, Elvis, Steve McQueen, James Dean, Clark Gable (who knew?), Roy Rogers, Arnold Schwarzenegger, Tim McGraw, and let's not forget the ladies: Cher, Tina Turner, Liz Taylor, Lauren Hutton, and I'm sure there are many more.

I can see parallels between the biker subculture and the cowboys of the American West and at the same time look forward to a future when more people might emulate the biker and unite in a brotherhood. Motorcycles bring people together. Riding unites you with other riders, whether they are professors or construction workers. Language experiences its limits in trying to describe what it's like to ride on a motorcycle.

So, as with the marble and the oil, the biker subculture evolved from an unexpected source – those veterans from WWII, the effects of war pushing those soldiers toward that sensation of being on a motorcycle that delivers what we're all seeking in life – Freedom – and our own personal Peace.

~

* BOYS WHO LIKE NOISE AND GIRLS WHO DON'T LIKE PEARLS *

~

Maybe it starts when they're around five years old. He is watching his favorite cartoon or TV show and suddenly he is captivated by the car chase and all the stuff being blown up on the screen. He turns up the volume because he likes how that screeching car sounds. After the show, the Matchbox cars come out and are lined up all over the living room. He imitates the car chase he just saw, accompanied by the relative noises. When he discovers Star Wars, around seven or eight, life is once again filled with noise – this time the sound of light sabers and Darth Vader. This must be how the obsession with noise begins. My son, now 11 years old, cannot let his father leave on the bike until he takes a turn twisting the throttle, just to hear the engine roar. Could this have anything to do with why so many guys modify their bikes to make them LOUDER? Hmmm, interesting thought.

What about the little girls who have absolutely no interest in Barbie dolls and would rather take their brother's Big Wheel for a spin around the yard? She's not afraid to get dirty and loves to look for worms and mess up anthills. Ribbons and pearls are not her first priority. There is a set of twins in my son's class who are cute and feminine, always wear pretty dresses, etc., but both of them can play as hard as the boys and handle a baseball bat just as well. Of course there are exceptions to every rule but obviously there are some qualities in kids that make you wonder if their destiny is already determined.

Next time a pack of bikers rides through town, notice who is lined up on the streets with the big grins on their faces, waving at the bikers and hoping their parents are aware of their excitement (for future reference). Watch your children – they may be fated to be weekend warriors!

~

BIG JOHN
* Powerful *

"I was 24 when I moved to Florida so I'd be able to ride year-round. I had a job, a place to live, and a few friends I had met, but my old crew was back in Massachusetts. When I met the Warlocks, I saw what I had at home, but more: BROTHERS who would have your back any time, day or night, guys to fight, fuck and ride motorcycles with, a home, and a brotherhood that I still believe in today. I still believe in the basics of the club - brothers and riding Harley-Davidsons!!"

Big John is the National President of the Warlocks Motorcycle Club, one of the largest and most notorious clubs in the world. I met John at his brother's first anniversary party of the Warlocks Hudson Valley Chapter in June of 2010. John lives up to his name. He's a big guy, tall, dark, handsome, and covered with tattoos. Although his appearance suggests a strong air of intimidation, I sensed a quiet intensity that was just as strong, along with a seemingly dark and brooding temperament. John commands respect not only by virtue of his position within the club, but because of his noticeable presence when he is in a crowd. John and his brother Ernie were born in Tewksbury, Massachusetts, but after the fire at their house, moved to their grandparents' home in Wilmington, the next town over. John

currently lives in Cocoa Beach, Florida. He moved to Florida for
the year-round riding.

~

**"I am a professional truck and heavy equipment
mechanic, and I own a small motorcycle shop where I
work after the day job. I am not married and have no
kids, never wanted them, even when I was young. It never
crossed my mind that I wanted to raise a family."**

~

John spends most of his time working as a mechanic or
managing his shop. Since he is not married with children, his
free time is spent living his life with the Warlocks. Not having
to commit to a wife may well be the reason he is able to devote
so much of himself to the club and I'm sure contributes to his
effectiveness as their National President. I am not privy to the
multitude of issues John must surely have to deal with, but
judging by the number of Warlocks chapters around the country
and the world, I assume his advice and expertise is sought on a
daily basis, and that there are always members to consult with
or confront and conflicts to resolve. Add to this the necessity
for John to travel around the country to meet or party with his
brothers and one realizes quickly just how much of his life is
consumed by the club. Riding to Sturgis in 2007, on the road for
nine days with his brothers, is one of John's priceless memories.

~

**"I was seven years old when I rode on a bike for the first
time. It was a 1971 Arctic Cat mini bike. My two aunts
each had one also, so we burnt up the area, man they
were fun!! That bike was also my first wreck, hit a large
pine tree root, the bike flew into the air, the front forks
came off and when it landed, it flung me face first into a
very large pine tree, man did that shit hurt...."**

How many bikers can say their first ride was at seven years
old?! Yes, it was a mini bike but apparently that was all it took
for John to get the riding gene flowing through his blood. Since
then, John has had six bikes: 1976 Harley-Davidson (HD) FXE,
1985 HD FXST, 1987 HD FXR, 1993 HD FLHS, 2005 HD FLRKI,

and he currently rides a 2007 HD Road Glide.   John does the mechanical work on all of his bikes.

~

"The morning my home burned down, I lost my mother and two younger brothers at the age of seven. I watched almost everything I knew go up in smoke, not knowing what had happened, where my family was, holding my little brother (just two years old at the time) who my mother had just passed to me though a second story window, waiting for my dad to get home from work and tell me what, why, how, where... It has left me cold in my adult days. Death, or I should say the death of other people, has no affect on me whatsoever. When I lose a club brother, I can't shed a tear for him because I have already seen enough death to last a lifetime."

John has experienced more at the age of seven than most people do throughout their entire life. For such a young child to survive a horrific house fire is a major catastrophe in itself, but to lose his mother and brothers at the same time had to be a tragedy beyond comprehension. Yet John had the courage to save his little brother while watching his family and everything he owned perish. It is no wonder he feels indifferent toward death.   How would a child of seven ever overcome such a nightmare? I guess that if one were in John's company often enough, they might see a hint of the sadness of that day still in his eyes. Your family at that age is all you know, they are your world, and John's loss had to be devastating to him and those who survived.

~

"I've always tried to be a good man, I see the good in people till they prove me wrong, and sometimes that does backfire on me - to let someone inside your circle only to find he's a scumbag who steals from you when you would have given him anything. Nothing scares me, but as I get older I value my life a little more. I also fear losing my own father; he's a great man, a great dad, and a great friend."

John speaks of his father with great admiration and respect. His father naturally had to raise his sons after the fire which I'm sure is why John and his brother developed such a close relationship with him. To grow up without a mother had to be the cause of much heartache, some of which will never heal. John does have some happy memories of his childhood; one is walking down the street to meet his father on his way home from work and riding in his 1961 Pontiac Catalina convertible. It was safe in those days for a child to walk a couple of blocks without adult supervision. John's dad, now retired, worked for a large northeast supermarket chain, and also worked with house framing to learn how to build a house for his family. These days, his father is a "snowbird," spending the winter in Florida and the summer in Massachusetts near his son Ernie and his children. John Sr. attends as many Warlocks MC events as possible and has always supported his children's endeavors.

~

"I graduated from a vocational high school (to learn diesel and heavy equipment repair). I was mechanically inclined already, having learned to work on cars and bikes at a young age, and I wanted to work on big trucks, still do!"

It seems John was almost groomed to be in the business he is now. It's not often that someone who chooses an occupation at the high school level will keep their interest through the years. He is fortunate in that respect; to be able to make a living working in the industry he loves.

~

"I've been clean and sober since 1996, before then a different story – I couldn't drink without snorting dope, couldn't snort dope without drinking. I was very lucky to have never wrecked or gotten a DUI because of alcohol."

John's problem with drugs and alcohol prior to 1996, I suspect, would have been a means to escape what must have been a sometimes very lonely adulthood, haunted by bittersweet memories of his mother and brothers, and of the future that was taken from them. No wonder John has no faith in God. However, there comes a time in everyone's life when you confront the man in the mirror and are forced to decide whether you are willing to live the rest of your life with a "monkey" on your back or if you have the strength to change that destiny. John chose change and now lives free of the tumultuous effects of substance abuse. With absolutely no regrets at this stage of his life, John does have one wish: ***"I always wanted to be able to fly a plane or a helicopter, just fly around and look at the land we walk on, until then, there's Google Earth..."***

~

"The night I got stabbed in the left armpit, I wasn't sure if the drive to the hospital was EVER going to end. My lung was collapsing and it was very hard to breathe, but I walked into the ER on my own. The expressions on people's faces were fucking priceless!!"

John has seen his share of death and almost lost his own life at 33. This man has been unwillingly perched on the edge of several cliffs but is always spared at the last minute. His purpose on this Earth is not complete. John believes wisdom comes with age and experience and this gels with his choice of "Unforgiven" with Clint Eastwood as his favorite movie of all time. Those who have seen "Unforgiven" may glimpse a better perception of John's character, while studying William Munny.

~

"I do feel more alive when riding in the mountains of West Virginia and anyplace new I haven't been before."

Big John travels around the country on his bike and has met hundreds, perhaps thousands, of Warlocks and other bikers on the road. He takes the time to speak with his Warlocks MC brothers and knows how crucial it is for him to be present, no matter the distance. His loyalty is appreciated by the Warlocks MC Nation. Although his presidential "duties" have taken a toll on him, John maintains his spirit of brotherhood toward the club and wouldn't have it any other way. He is, however, "old school," and would like to see more of the larger clubs embrace the original ideals which were the foundation of the first motorcycle clubs in America. Perhaps, under John's leadership, those ideals will resurface in years to come, at least within the Warlocks Motorcycle Club.

John feels that clubs are losing their old-school values for several reasons. One reason is that the people who should be passing down the values are younger and the old-timers just get lost on the younger generation's thoughts and attitudes. Another is a double-edged sword: in the past, when clubs were always fighting, members had to depend on their brothers and their lives were in each other's hands. That fact is not true today. Too many join to be cool; they don't put their heart and soul into it like bikers did twenty, thirty, forty years ago, etc.

~

"Being in a one-percenter motorcycle club isn't easy. It isn't what the club can do for you, it's what can you do for your club. Always stick to the basics of the club, riding and brotherhood. The club isn't there for drugs, stealing motorcycles, getting drunk and causing trouble, it's there because brothers before you lived for brotherhood. Always keep the brotherhood alive, too many large clubs have lost that. I put my heart and soul into being a Warlock!"

BIG JOHN

* CLUB INTIMIDATION *

~

Although this is an interpretation by this author of the world we live in, the tale this story tells is about the perception of intimidation among bikers at a particular motorcycle event. While "hanging out" with some club members, more than a few daggers could be felt from the surrounding bikers who seemed a little uncomfortable with the fact that these clubbers were around. For the purpose of this essay, the term "biker" will mean any biker and the term "clubber" will mean a club member. It is understandable, to some extent, that cliques do still exist, whether in high school or in the real world; however, some bikers clearly frowned upon the presence of the clubbers in a territorial kind of way.

Stand before a biker the same way you stand before a clubber and you are usually treated the same way. I never feel threatened by these men, contrary to that, I actually feel safer around them. To a clubber there are brothers, there are other bikers, and there are women. We are more or less treated equally by bikers and clubbers. The difference is that with clubbers, their brothers are treated better than equally, and that is how it should be. Brothers to them are family. No doubt it is the "straight shooting" characteristic about clubbers that sets them apart. They do seem to display an air of superiority wherever they go, or is that just imagined? Are you not proud when you arrive somewhere surrounded by your family members?

The bikers were unfairly discriminating against their own kind. The guys in the club are still bikers. Why not accept them and welcome them into your own world? It does not matter if the club is Outlaw, Christian, or a Motorcycle or Riding club. We all demand and deserve respect. A few bikers could be heard mocking the names of clubs and the notion of prospecting. How dare anyone judge the club structure without understanding it? There are reasons for everything that happens within a club and the fact that clubs have survived as long as they have is solid testament to the fact that the structure works.

The biker world is a good place to learn lessons in honor, respect, and humility and we could all benefit. Though a club member may live a life very different from our own, that is perfectly acceptable and they still deserve our respect. To those of you who disagree, I respect your opinion but you'll find me all over the playground, in all the sandboxes, even the ones with the patches!

~

* DO YOU WANNA' GO TO A REAL PARTY? *

~

Many people in the Capital District of New York are unaware of the mere existence of motorcycle clubs. Naturally, if you are not interested in motorcycles and/or are not involved in the biker community, then you may not ever come in contact with anyone associated with a motorcycle club. Most people, though, biker or not, know of the club known as the Harley Owner's Group, otherwise known as HOG. HOG events are usually exclusive to HOG members and that is fine. However, how many of you are aware that most of the other motorcycle clubs in the community, outlaw and otherwise, host events throughout the year and those events are *open to the public*? This means that you, your mother, and your grandparents are invited to attend. When you read "ALL are welcome," that is exactly what it means. Club parties are not just for club members.

Yes, there will be a requested donation, which covers your admission to the event (or ride), and the food that is usually served during the event. There are times of course that the admission fee, or a percentage of it, will go to whatever charity or organization for which the event is held. People arrive on bikes or in cars and once they enter the venue, are greeted by the hosts and welcomed to the party. A lot of mingling takes place and almost everyone leaves with at least one new friend. Chances are you already have the most important thing in common – a love for riding – which makes enough of a foundation to begin a new acquaintance.

Bikers may have the reputation of being major party people, and that may be true, but that doesn't mean that the clerk at the local convenience store or the head nurse at your town's hospital can't join in the fun. We are all the same when it comes to enjoying life – if it feels good, we are damn well going to do it (or at least try)! Sure, there will be the occasional scuffle here and there, but bikers for the most part "police" themselves and do everything they can to prevent problems or stain the reputation

of their club.   Before learning all about the motorcycle club
community in the Northeast, this author was content just to
attend a house party now and then, but since then have found
myself at every biker event thinking exactly as Jack did in the
movie *Titanic*, when he whisked Rose away from the mundane
dinner party, to the REAL party down in the lower decks. Venture
out to a club party in your area – you will be glad you took the
plunge!

~

BIG MIKE
* Conviction *

"I judge everyone the same until they prove me wrong."

Mike is a man of many convictions. He is ruled by his convictions in most cases and this is admired by his close friends and family members. Mike grew up in Lynn, Massachusetts, loving the close proximity of the ocean and all that goes along with life near the sea. For several years, Mike ran a fishing boat with his cousin from Maine, fishing for lobster along the New England coast and enjoying a life shared with fresh air, sunshine, and endless sunrises and sunsets. Lobster fishing along the New England coast is highly competitive and can be very difficult. Mike's boat was docked in Gloucester (yes, where "The Perfect Storm" was filmed, in fact Mike approached George Clooney on the set and said hello during a break in the filming). He and his cousin would set out for two to three days at a time, hoping for a good catch so they could arrive back home with enough earnings to take care of their families.

~

*"I have a good sense of humor but
I am serious when necessary."*

Writing about Mike is easy because I know him so well. Having spent time with Mike over the past few years, we have become close friends and I've learned a lot about the man under the green hat. Mike is extremely intelligent and has many talents that are hidden from most of his peers, either because he wants it that way, or because his modesty keeps him from revealing it. We have had conversations for hours, discussing every topic under the sun. We have shared some heartache and cried together but we have also laughed so hard at times that we would double over from the emotion. He has a wicked sense of humor. One time, when he asked me to watch his dog, Mini, while he was out of town, he called to ask what I had fed her. I replied, "Well, I kinda' gave her a sandwich." I thought he would die from laughing so hard (how did I know dogs don't eat sandwiches)!

Mike is a caring, compassionate, and considerate friend. I may treat Mike to McDonalds. Mike in turn will "repay" me by making me shrimp and lobster! There was a time when I drank too much while in his company. Later he asked me, with an "I told you so" tone: "So when and what do you think you did wrong?" I would not have made it through that incident so well without Mike's help. He assumed responsibility for my well-being and I was grateful that he was there. I always feel safe and protected when I'm with Mike. He is a man who takes the words "love" and "friendship" very seriously.

Besides spending part of his life as a fisherman, Mike worked for GE (General Electric, a major power company) in Massachusetts, as a Machinist, for 16 years, until an accident on the job forced him into retirement. He then drove a truck for a few years but was involved in a serious accident and as a result became disabled and unable to work. Mike also suffers from a form of muscular dystrophy and is in constant pain.

~

"I think I am a damn good father."

Mike was married once and has a son, now 25, living with his mother in Massachusetts. Although time and distance keeps him from seeing his son very often, Mike is in constant contact with him and is a good father. He spent years coaching Joey in baseball and, as manager, led the team for several years, finishing in the top of their division as Lynn City Champs.

~

"I think I was about 10 years old when I rode a motorcycle for the first time. I built my first bike, a 1957 Harley-Davidson, when I was 20. I regret selling that bike."

Mike's father was a hard-working man, but he was also very selfish. For whatever reasons, his father was most likely angry at himself and that anger was spilled onto his wife and sons for many years. His father was not a man who lovingly guided his children. Instead, he would expect Mike and his brothers, when they were very young, to help him with construction projects needed to be done around the house, or to work at the food concession they owned at a local race track. Even though Mike felt a lot of bitterness toward his father, he does credit him for teaching him and encouraging his mechanical ability. His dad also loved and owned a few antique cars and I think Mike also shares that trait. Mike believes his best qualities came from his mother. He knows how strong she had to have been to endure a difficult life with his father, and still be able to love and nurture her sons on her own. He regrets not spending more time with his mother before she died.

Mike built his own bike, a 1957 Harley-Davidson, at 20 years old, using his mechanical talent and teaching himself everything he needed to know to build a custom motorcycle. Mike rode that bike for 11 years up and down the east coast, mostly in New England.

With his mechanical mind, Mike is able to fix just about anything after studying it for a few minutes, then taking it apart and putting it back together! If he can't figure it out initially, you can be damn sure Mike will seek a solution to the problem any way he can. Mike also learned the art of tattooing (mostly self-taught), and practiced that art whenever he was able. Although he does not consider himself a professional in this area, he has done very well and has produced some amazing ink on his subjects. In fact, I commissioned him to ink my first tattoo, a symbol from the *Phantom of the Opera,* and I absolutely love it.

~

"I've been riding all my life and really loved the history of the Boozefighters."

Mike is a member of the Boozefighters Motorcycle Club (Mountain Chapter 60). His chapter is based in Troy, New York, and Mike was initiated into the club in 2008, after moving to New York from Massachusetts in 2006. Mike is the most "traditional" club member I have met in the years I've been around bikers. He believes strongly in adhering to the bylaws of his club and tries to encourage his brothers to do the same. Mike has proudly served as Sgt. at Arms and President of the Boozefighters Chapter 60. His commitment to the club through some trials and tribulations is commendable.

~

"Losing my brother in a motorcycle accident as a teenager changed my life, but every death I hear about, whether family or friends, affects me deeply."

Mike has shared stories with me about his brother, Joey, and his mother. Mike was a teenager when Joey was killed in a motorcycle accident. He was heartbroken, lost, and couldn't understand how God could take someone so young who he loved so much. Joey was his best friend. The family dynamic changed and his parents were never the same following Joey's death. His father, already a hard-hearted man, grew even more cold and distant. Mike's teenage years were full of pain and resentment. His father was no comfort to the family and his mother bore the burden of keeping him and his older brother from breaking down and helped them move forward with their lives. She shielded them from most of their father's selfish tantrums and carried them through their grief. To honor his brother's memory, Mike named his son after Joey.

~

"I don't go to church or pray as much as I should but I do believe in God."

Mike loves to talk about his mother. He remembers how loving and supportive she was to him and how much she suffered for her children. Mike keeps a box full of memories of his mother. Recipes, photographs, and other mementos remind him of the wonderful, caring woman she was, despite the struggles she went through with his father. I feel as if I knew his mother after hearing him speak of her so often.

Mike is an animal lover and advocate, owns a little miniature pinscher dog named Mini, and treats her like a daughter, sometimes even going without food himself so that he can feed Mini. He is outspoken when it comes to matters of politics or issues affecting the community, the state, or the world, and he can be quick to anger at the ignorance of politicians and people who don't have care or compassion for others.

Perhaps the reason Mike and I have such a good rapport and "hit it off" so well is because we are both individuals with many diverse interests. There is a stubborn streak in him, but it never keeps him from compromising when necessary or admitting failure and taking responsibility for his actions. Love, respect, and loyalty are very important to Mike, and even though he would walk a mile with aching feet or suffer some hardship to visit or help a friend, he never expects anything in return. In fact, he is often humbled by any exchange he receives.

~

"I fear the day I can't ride anymore...there are no words to describe what it's like to feel that freedom."

Because of his muscle disease, Mike is very aware that his body may not be strong enough in future years to enable him to continue riding. Riding may be the only diversion Mike has that allows him, even for just awhile, to forget his disability. Mike's passion for riding is such that his motorcycle is often his primary means of transportation throughout the year. I have had the privilege of riding with Big Mike and it is quite an experience. He's a wild man when he feels the "need for speed," but he is so skilled at riding that I felt completely safe, and he knows when to slow down. He is also extremely cautious. As long as I've known Mike, I have never seen him drive under the influence of drugs or alcohol.

~

"I would love to ride in the space shuttle."

He doesn't look to his friends or seem like the adventurous type but Mike is very much a risk-taker and would not hesitate to learn or try something new (our trips to the grocery store taught me that). I am not surprised that he would jump at the chance to travel to space.

~

"Enjoy life, we are not here long!"

Mike is a man of many talents, but a man of few words. If he is engaged in captivating conversation, however, he will debate for hours with a partner. Mike owns a silent strength that is unfortunately hidden from most people by a mask of humbleness, removed only when he reaches a level of trust with a person. I admire his compassion, his perceptiveness, his survival instincts (emotional and physical), and the intuitiveness he seems to have for the needs of his friends. I am proud to know and love this fascinating, reserved, man of humility and convictions, my dear friend and "brother," Mike Mazza.

~

"Wisdom comes from age, experience, keeping your eyes and ears open, and keeping your mouth shut."

BIG MIKE

* A BIKER'S HEART *

~

You are going to have "bad apples" in every culture you study; there is no doubt about that. In my own experience, though, it seems there is more heart and soul in the biker culture than any other. More heartache, more heartbreak, but also more heartfelt love and affection. These passions are more pronounced. Bikers have stepped up to offer time, energy, and money to charities or to help someone in need, whether it is a fellow biker, or a child suffering from a disease or other misfortune.

Watch the exchange between a biker and his partner and you will notice that they are usually very much "in tune" with each other. They have to be, after all, to ride together on a motorcycle. That is very personal, as in a sense you are trusting the driver with your life, and that takes a lot of faith in each other. Biker breakups are usually pretty volatile (the hotter the fire, the more explosive). On the other hand, those in love will be the most loyal and devoted, and yes, typically more protective, of each other.

I attended a "biker baby shower," and although there was no indication of how many would show up for the party (because, as someone said, "Come on, bikers don't RSVP, they just show up!"), indeed they showed up, ironically, in *packs*, to shower the mother with gifts. It was like walking into a surprise party within a party. To the other extreme, a biker friend of the community died suddenly and the bikers who came to show their respect and support may well have been the larger "family" in attendance. There are "clean and sober" clubs who have stepped in to "save" a fellow biker struggling with alcohol or drug addiction, a daunting task for *anyone* to attempt.

Regardless of how often we see bikers organizing or participating in charity fundraisers, we are still amazed at how many really care and take the time to do something about it. It is wonderful to witness a room full of bikers, male and female, with hearts bigger than their saddlebags!

~

* PIANOS AND
MOTORCYCLES *

~

Aren't we all interested in how things are made? After all, there had to be enough curiosity out there for television shows to be produced, providing us with the inside information about the intricate details necessary to create whatever is being showcased. Having toured a piano factory recently, I now have a much clearer understanding of how a piano works, how the keys produce a note, and how the 2,500 or so pieces that go into building a piano all work together to achieve the most harmonious sound possible. You can get a vague idea of what's involved in the construction of a piano by a simple internet search, but it's not the same as being there and witnessing the process firsthand. It has actually given me a deeper appreciation for the instrument and, ironically, I feel more intimately involved with my own piano.

Of course I've seen the motorcycle build shows on TV. My husband, Dino Petrocelli, has been featured on American Chopper more than once and still works with Paul Jr., so watching them build bikes is nothing new. However, now I realize that none of that will mean anything to me unless or until I watch someone build a bike right in front of me. I am more interested in the riders of motorcycles, but this experience has made me wonder whether those bikers who adore their machines are the ones who have participated in building their own. It would surprise me if that was not the case.

Learning about the process of constructing a piano, particularly a grand piano, has reaffirmed my wish for a baby grand, and my respect for this incredible instrument is greater than ever. Still, the piano, like the motorcycle, can only "sing" with the most passionate "player." Find a bike builder who will let you stand by and watch him work, or, if you are so inclined, try to build one yourself. Anyone who owns a motorcycle should learn how they work – surely the result *will* be a more passionate "player," a rider who truly feels at one with his machine.

~

BROADWAY LEE
* Old-School *

"Be true to yourself, everyone else is taken, and you can't change the past!"

Lee Sikes is the proud owner of Broadway Choppers, located at 1518 Bradley Street in Schenectady, New York, now in its fifteenth year of service to motorcyclists in the tri-city area (Albany, Schenectady, Troy) and beyond. While attending his first Laconia rally and judging one of the bike shows there, Lee and his partner at the time were inspired and decided that when they arrived back home, they would work to establish a motorcycle shop.

I first met Lee at my husband's photography studio while he was there for a photo shoot. Lee is friendly, very personable, and has an "old-school" air about him. Maybe it's his handsome boyish looks or his mischievous smile that contributes to his charm; whatever it is, one is immediately at ease around Lee. When I stop to see Lee at his shop, I'm quite sure I could talk to him for hours and about anything. If you're a friend to Lee, he is totally engaged when you are together. One of the things I love about him is that from the beginning of our friendship, he has always made me feel like a sister. Lee has supported Dino and me in many of our endeavors and we try to do the same for him.

~

"My son, Dylan, has dwarfism, and I worry about his future health needs in this cold world, as well as my daughter, who has a heart of gold, dealing with the same cold world!"

Lee is married to the love of his life, Manon, and they have two children together, "Princess" Bianca and Dylan, AKA DoubleD, who was born with dwarfism. It is easy to see how passionate he is about his family, as his smile radiates around him when he is relating stories about his wife and children. Lee was always very involved with his children, from changing diapers to attending every school function. He never misses the "real moments" in their lives. He's also naturally protective of his kids and worries about their future, as any father would, especially in regard to his son and his handicap. From what I have seen, there will be no problems because Lee and Manon are extremely loving parents who know how important it is to instill self-confidence and strength in their kids, despite any perceived disability.

~

"I am aware of how serious it is to be a father and I am grateful to know unconditional love...I am so concerned about their future..."

Lee is one of the first in the biker community to offer his help at charity biker events, or more often, to take the reins on the project himself and organize the entire benefit. One of the events he coordinated was a ride to benefit the Ronald McDonald House, which drew a lot of media attention, and included bikers from our community as well as local politicians. He participates in several biker benefits for children who are seriously ill, taking time from his busy schedule to do all he can to achieve a successful outcome. He draws a crowd simply because his friends know his heart is in everything he does, and he is admired for his efforts and the time and energy he lends to those occasions.

Loyalty is a priority to Lee and those who are lucky to share his friendship know that he can be called upon whenever he is needed. However, once he is crossed, the bridge may never be rebuilt. This might be a harsh reality about Lee, but it is the way he chooses to live his life. He may forgive but he will never forget.

~

"I was about six or seven when my grandfather said to me, "Look at you and your skinny legs, what the hell, you better eat more vegetables and get tuff or you're never gonna' get nowhere in this world!" My grandfather died not too long after telling me that. When I was near the end of my Marine Corps boot camp at Paris Island, the senior drill instructor called me into his office to inform me that not only was I graduating boot camp and becoming a United States Marine, but I was getting meritoriously promoted to Private First Class! I could hear my grandfather's voice that day and I realized then that he probably knew he wasn't gonna' be around and wanted to make sure I was tuff enough. I will love that fact forever! THAT'S OLD-SCHOOL LOVE."

For as long as he can remember, ("forever" he says), Lee has been interested in motorcycles, which is a good thing, since he has made them his life's work. He is no stranger to the streets and has been riding for 30 years now, *maybe* a little less since having been transplanted from Miami about 16 years ago! It would be hard to find a businessman in the biker community who socializes with more people or participates in more charity (and non-charity) biker events than Lee. *"It's not just what I do, it's who I am."* Lee Sikes is the reason his business has been so successful in this area. Lee and his wife, Manon, both ride their own bikes and are very active in the biker community. Lee is a valuable member of our biker community for several reasons. One is his business of course, servicing many of the bikers in the Albany area, and the other is his dedication to helping local charities. Lee is always motivated to rally everyone together for a good cause or just to gather friends for a ride. He even hosted a Customer Appreciation Day in 2010, treating all of his customers, family, and friends to a free BBQ and a day full of fun events. He values his customers and likes to "give back" when he can.

Lee is known to craft trophies or other keepsakes from motorcycle parts. These one-of-a-kind creations have been used as prizes in bike shows, or even as gifts. This is another example of Lee's artistic talent. Carmella Brown, from *New York Rider*

Magazine, asked him once to create something that she would be able to give to someone who was visiting from California and attending the New York City motorcycle show. Within just a few days, Lee delivered a unique motorcycle piece which we proudly presented to our friend to take home. She was thrilled and honored to receive the hand-made gift.

~

"I was about eight years old the first time I rode on a motorcycle. I remember the day very, very well, on the back of my Uncle Terry's chopper around my grandmother's neighborhood. My mother said, 'Oh no, that's my brother's bike and he's wild!' Of course we got busted by them. Uncle Terry still rides."

Lee's ideas for designing the bikes come from spending time "in the wind" and of course from customers who know what they want and special order from Lee. His customers know that if they want their bike built (or customized) the right way, Broadway Choppers will take care of it. Lee takes his time and spends an average of 150 hours on each bike, which takes a lot of the headache off the customer's shoulders! No motorcycle will leave the shop until it is complete and in perfect condition. Lee looks forward to continued success as long as high quality becomes possible. Lee's plans for the future of Broadway Choppers include someday moving into a larger building with room for expansion. He also envisions the possibility of sharing his shop with a tattoo artist as well as offering a "chopper" product line to his customers.

~

"Live life like a camera is on you - Actions speak louder than words!"

Lee is what most would define as a "straight shooter," who does not mix words. He is confident in his work and is a progressive thinker in terms of his business. Lee surrounds himself with people who have earned his trust and respect and those qualities are among the most valuable to him. Lee is not a superficial man and has a keen sense for realizing a person's true motives. If he feels a threat or betrayal is imminent, he will confront the problem and deal with it head on. He is brutally honest with people. If for some reason he has distanced himself from someone, everyone will know it. There is no hiding behind any masks with Lee. What you see is what you get and what you sow is what you reap.

Even though Lee is a gentleman, he can also be hot-headed. However, he is wise enough to know that decisions made out of anger can backfire and result in more discord. He knows he must remind himself that he is a businessman and needs to protect those interests. Lee has a good rapport with his competitors in the industry, realizing that this world is big enough for all of us. Lee enjoys long and loyal friendships with local club members, and is respected by those who know him.

~

"I regret taking so long to think with my head instead of my heart."

Practicality can halt creativity. Lee, at this point in his life, has learned the value of following instincts and taking chances. He's not one to squander his small fortune; instead he prefers to share his success whenever possible. He is a generous man with a heart of gold, and welcomes new friends and the ventures to come. Time offers us wisdom with every life lesson, and Lee believes he has only begun to realize his potential. He is optimistic about the future and what lies on his horizon.

There is no doubt in my mind that Lee will be successful in all his endeavors, both personal and professional, and I am proud and honored to call him a friend.

~

"Giving someone what they have not earned is like pouring sand into their hands."

BROADWAY LEE

* WHAT KIND OF PEOPLE RIDE MOTORCYCLES? *

~

My son, when he was 8-years-old, asked me what kind of people can ride motorcycles. I thought, now that is an interesting question for a young man who is accustomed to seeing his own parents on a motorcycle. Then I thought of his question as an opportunity to open up a broader dialogue with him so that even at his young age, I could possibly keep him from developing the usual misconceptions about bikers.

The simple answer is *anyone* can ride a motorcycle. No, you don't have to be rich, you don't have to be in a motorcycle club, you don't have to wear a leather jacket, and you don't even have to be a BOY! You can be a doctor or work in any other profession and ride a motorcycle, you can be a librarian, keeping as quiet as a mouse during the week, but roaring down the road on your bike on Saturdays. You can be a nun or a monk cloistered in a monastery somewhere and have a secret desire to ride a Harley. Motorcycles do not discriminate.

But what about the *kind* of person who rides a motorcycle? The kind of person who savors the feeling of the wind in their hair, or the smell of the grass in the summer is the kind of person who might ride a motorcycle. The man who feels as much love for his club brother as a family member is the kind of person who rides a motorcycle. The women I meet at biker events are generally free-spirited people who have no interest in comparing designer labels or talking about celebrities and their "reality" lives. They smile when they meet me and they listen to what I am saying, instead of sizing me up and thinking, wow, she could stand to lose a few pounds, or on the other hand, wondering if I'm any kind of threat to their world. I watch the guys at biker events, and I see their genuine concern when they ask each other how they've been or inquire about another brother.

I was at a motorcycle club party and was handed a flyer announcing an upcoming benefit event for a brother from another club who was struggling with cancer, not only physically and emotionally but also financially. When I sat down to read the flyer, I was moved, really moved, by the raw and unwritten emotions that this flyer represented. These are men who truly care about their fellow man, a biker "brother" -- enough to *act* on that concern and assume some guardianship for his welfare. These guys know what the term "my brother's keeper" means.

I have encountered the most unlikely souls in the biker world, some lost, some searching, some already found, yet all with something very important in common: they live every moment of their lives with passion.

The person who values the real moments of his/her life, as well as the people who surround them with happiness, is the kind of person who rides a motorcycle. Like me, like him, like her, and yes, son, maybe *you* someday.

~

* BIKES VS. BAGS *

~

Why does a guy buy a Harley, bring it home from the shop, and immediately start thinking of things to change on the bike? Maybe even *before* he makes the purchase, when he's just shopping around and looking at bikes, the wheels are turning in his mind about replacing the pipes and how to change the handlebars, etc. The wife gets a little irritated, considering he just spent part of the savings they were supposed to use to renovate the kitchen and here he is adding to the tab already. But then she turns around and grabs one of her designer bags, slings it over her shoulder and follows the Mister out to the bike to take a ride on over to the dealership just to look around. While he's over there looking at the parts and accessories, she wanders over to the motor clothes area to check out the new shirts and stuff. She sees a nice black leather bag that catches her eye and she goes to investigate. Yeah, nice, but it's no Prada.

I am finding it increasingly difficult to find no-name pocketbooks in department stores these days. Bummer for me since I was never a designer-bag-type woman. I just don't want to pay the price. But I do understand the desire for certain characteristics on bags, just like the biker who wants to personalize his bike. Number one on the agenda always seems to be the pipes. The pipes need to be changed – why? "To make the bike louder," he says. Now why would the bike have to be made louder than it already is? Hmmm... And then some pipes just look cooler than others (fishtail, etc.) Next comes the transformation of the handlebars. I haven't seen a man yet who will settle for stock handlebars. For whatever reason, they have to be altered in some way – to straight bars, ape hangers, etc. Then of course we need custom foot pegs and mirrors, maybe a sharp looking kickstand. Of course the seat will definitely have to be replaced. He needs something more comfortable and must either add a sissy bar for the wife or take off the one that came with it. Last but not least, we need a totally new paint job. Can't have a boring solid colored bike. We need flames, maybe

a tribal design, or a logo, or something. Anything. Just get a
new paint job.

As for me, the black rat bike up the street would be good
enough. As long as it serves the purpose, I'm happy. But for
others, it's custom all the way or nothing at all. And while
my pocketbook-partying friends continue to spend half their
paychecks on another designer bag, I'll settle for the no-name
conventional, heavy duty, practical bag for $25. (OK, I confess,
last week I bought myself a designer bag - just couldn't resist
the shiny pipes...oops I mean zippers). We all love our toys.

~

BROWNIE
* Fierce *

"Riding is in my blood, I've survived many "wipe-outs," but I keep riding."

Handsome Brownie! I have to begin with those two words since, besides being a member of the Leathernecks Motorcycle Club, Dennis Brown, aka Brownie, is well known for his extremely handsome features. Brownie's got the dark, brooding looks, the mannerisms, and everything about him exudes a strong masculinity that is irresistibly attractive to women. That is just one characteristic of Brownie, however, and hopefully his story will provide a little insight into this intriguing man.

Brownie's first experience on a motorcycle was when he was only six years old, riding a Bultaco 250 mini-bike! He had a 360 Honda when he was older and has owned several Harley-Davidson Road Kings over the years, as well as a Titan Chopper. He currently rides a 2005 Road King which he had painted to honor the Marine Corps, and he also owns a Harley-Davidson Deuce. Brownie has won 10 awards for his Marine Corps bike, including an award from the Hells Angels Motorcycle Club, presented to him one year at the Hells Angels Rumble on the River event.

Brownie was a "bad boy" in school when he was living in Minnesota, always getting into some kind of trouble, but when he was expelled in ninth grade for the umpteenth time; it was apparently the "last straw" for the local authorities. His mother was told that if Dennis didn't leave the state, he was going to be put into a juvenile home. Mom sent him back to Schenectady to live with his Uncle Carmen. Dennis actually did well in high school in Schenectady, became a football "star" and earned the name "Maddog." He graduated, then immediately enlisted in the Marines at 17 (through the "delayed enlistment program"), and entered military service at 18.

In 2009, I interviewed Brownie for an article which was to appear in *New York Rider Magazine*. During that time, Brownie was a member of the Boozefighters Motorcycle Club. He was featured, along with a young soldier, in the centerfold of the May issue. Brownie, a (23-year) retired Marine Veteran, lives in Latham, New York. We met at a local bar on a Tuesday afternoon, started talking over a beer and then decided to take a ride to pick up some pictures of his bike that he wanted to show me. While we were riding in the car, I asked him questions about his life, his family, etc., and he told me about his three children - his son, Dennis Jr., daughter Dyonne, and Dena Rosebud, the daughter he lost in 2005 to melanoma. He took the time to stop at the cemetery on the way to show me the memorial he had built in honor of his daughter, a marble bench inscribed with her name and a favorite passage that she loved. He recalled to me the day she was born while he was stationed at Camp Lejeune in 1975, and how happy he was to meet his newborn daughter. He brought Dena to life with his memories. I had the chance to admire the various medals he's earned from his 23-year military career, three years of active duty in the Marines, then 20 years in the U.S. Navy Seabees. One of Brownie's jobs as a Seabee was Service Military Instructor (S.M.I.), teaching hand to hand combat and combat tactics.

~

"The defining moments in my life were as a Marine in combat, losing my brothers, and losing the pride and joy of my life, my daughter, Dena Rosebud, to cancer."

Ever since he was a child, Brownie dreamed of joining the military. He was born in Schenectady, New York, raised in Minneapolis, Minnesota, and after working for his Uncle Carmen at the family tree farm for a few years, he enlisted in the Marines, and never looked back. Brownie has traveled extensively throughout his military career, including time in Cuba, Japan, Hawaii, and Guam. He served in the Gulf War (Desert Storm) in 1990, surviving some of the darkest days of his life with courage and dignity. He received the highest rank of "Expert" in handling an AR14 and AR16, as well as the M-50 and M-60 machine guns. I was grateful for how candid he was with me when talking about his life, his own self-judgment about his past, his mistakes, his triumphs, and the emotional and physical pain he carries. He bears his crosses well and willingly. Brownie is bold, confident and fierce if provoked, and under all of that keeps a sincere sense of caring and compassion for his comrades. I'm sure those who know him have noticed the old-fashioned sense of gallantry about him.

Brownie has the greatest respect for the soldiers, men and women, who bravely and proudly serve our military, especially during this time of turmoil. Brownie had decided years ago, after surviving a serious motorcycle crash, to honor the military by having his bike painted as a tribute to the U.S. Marine Corps. Brownie's military career is as much as part of his makeup as his genetics. He is a proud Marine and grew up in a traditional Italian family. I have had occasion to witness Brownie with other Marines and it is both inspiring and impressive to see the mutual respect and camaraderie.

~

"I am a Retired Marine and a proud member of the Leathernecks Motorcycle Club."

Many who think they know Brownie see a man who is charming and personable to everyone he meets, especially to women. Though he may be preoccupied with his brothers in the club, he never fails to take time to greet the females and leave them smiling. He simply slays us women with his charm, not to mention a smile that could melt a cold heart! Yet, despite all the women he's known in his life, he confesses that he's only truly been in love a couple of times. There is a man behind that brilliant smile who carries deep pain within his heart, but he will hide that pain behind a mask of bravado. You rarely catch him without that mask, but if you do, it's quite startling because Brownie's weak moments are few and far between.

~

"I was married twice, have two children now, and consider myself an excellent father. I regret not spending enough time with my daughter before she passed away."

Brownie's life changed most dramatically when he lost his daughter and that loss remains as potent as ever. There is no relief from the loss of your child, only a new "normal." Having known Brownie for a few years now, I am convinced that it is the love for his children and grandchildren that sustains him. Brownie is a devoted family man, and believes that, though he is now divorced, it is still his responsibility to care for his ex-wife. His other children, Dennis Jr. and Dyonne, are carefully protected by their father, and they know he will always be a strong presence in their lives. I recall an afternoon spent with Brownie during which he told me he was worried about his son. We had a nice lunch and talked about other things, but the majority of his time that day was spent on the phone with his son, encouraging him, and trying to resolve his child's latest dilemma. He spends as much time as possible with his children and grandchildren, and they are always his first priority. His love for his family has no bounds.

~

"I turn into a Demon and I'm out of control, sometimes black out!"

Brownie does have a dark side and that is evidenced by his temper. He freely admits that he has a hard time controlling his anger. That uncontrollable anger cost him dearly, however, when in a fit of "road-rage" while riding his motorcycle in 2007, he kicked in the door of a truck near him which was driven by a man who was apparently intoxicated, and interfering with Brownie and his friends. Brownie's legs were pinned under the truck when the driver swerved to avoid him at 55 mph, leaving Brownie under a guardrail. The Road King he was riding was totaled and his leg was seriously damaged. Brownie credits Chuck, a member of the 69ers Motorcycle Club, and Chuck's wife Robin, also riding with Brownie that day, for saving his life, since they were the first to help when he opened his eyes after the accident. Brownie spent six months in the hospital, endured three surgeries over the course of three years, and was fitted with a fixater for his leg to keep the fractured bones stabilized and in alignment.   Unfortunately, Brownie's leg did not stay in alignment and the bone curved as it healed. A few years later, Brownie faced the difficult decision of enduring major surgery to restore his leg as much as possible to its original condition. His chances of success were 50/50 – the operation would either be successful or he would lose the leg. Days before the surgery, I asked him if he was scared or apprehensive and whether he had any second thoughts. He said, "Absolutely not. I know the risk and I am taking it." His doctor had to re-break the leg, extract a bone out of his hip and insert rods and a plate into his leg, which required an eight-hour surgery. Brownie emerged from the ordeal with a complete recovery and now enjoys life without the cane he was forced to use for so many years. His bravery during that time taught me a lot about him. Brownie does not know fear. He has been close to death many times in his life and fear does not exist in his world.

~

"I am not afraid of death, in fact, I welcome it, as long as I can go out doing my thing - protecting, riding, or just living life on the edge!"

Some may view Brownie's volatile temper as a fault; on the contrary, I admire his determination to fight viciously for justice, especially for people and principles he holds dear. *"I would kill a terrorist who was planning to kill Americans. I would want to kill him with my bare hands."* With a desire to make things right with a world in turmoil, the soldier in Brownie would have no qualms about fighting for his country, even at this stage of his life. He loves the freedom of riding, loves being out in the "elements," and sometimes considers riding his necessary "therapy."

As a club member, Brownie is a good "soldier," and loyal to his brothers, never wavering in his allegiance. He may not always agree with club decisions, but he understands and accepts whatever doctrines are established. Brownie is currently the Sgt. at Arms of the Leathernecks Motorcycle Club (Empire) and he serves in that role with pride. He is a worthy representative for his club, as he also was as a member of the Boozefighters

MC. Brownie loves the camaraderie and the brotherhood he feels from being a club member.

~

"I'm up front and real, and I love my family and my brothers."

Brownie has been a treasured friend to me since our first meeting. One reason is because he is a "paisan" and we've spent many hours talking and laughing about our Italian heritage. More precious to me though, are the times we've spent sharing some wine, Johnny Cash and Frank Sinatra! I have shared some trials and tribulations with Brownie and he has shown deep concern for my welfare, with encouraging words and his assurance that our friendship is sealed beyond a casual relationship. He follows through on his promises and leaves no stones unturned. I truly believe he would "take a bullet" for me, as he probably would for any of his close friends. I am grateful for the connection we have together and he has touched my heart with his love and loyalty.

~

"Live to ride, dead or alive!"

BROWNIE

* WHAT DO ALL THOSE PATCHES MEAN? *

~

There is literally no end to the variation of patches that can be seen on the vests of bikers at any motorcycle event. What do all those patches mean and where do they come from?

The patches signify membership but they are not like Girl or Boy Scout patches which you earn from performing good deeds or accomplishing a task. Actually, that is not entirely true. Biker patches *are* earned through an accomplishment. That accomplishment is typically the result of a year (or more) of major commitment and hard work. Membership patches can signify membership in a riding club, an outlaw club, or an independent rider club (such as a local group of riding buddies who want to form a club and design their own patch, write their own bylaws, etc.)

So what is the difference between a Riding Club (RC) and a Motorcycle Club (MC)? In a riding club, the patch is usually bought, not earned, and is owned by the person who wears it. Riding club patches are usually one-piece patches depicting the name of the club. Motorcycle club patches almost always consist of three-piece patches – a top patch (also called a "rocker") with the name of the club. The center patch is the logo of the club, and the bottom rocker will reveal the geographical location of the club or a quote or statement exclusive to that club. Each piece of the patch is earned independently and denotes another "step" into the club. Naturally, it is much more of a commitment to belong to a motorcycle club than to a riding club and the same goes for earning the patches. Since the patch is earned, after a period of prospecting in a motorcycle club, that patch is owned by the club, not the individual. This is why the man who wears an MC patch is called a patch *holder*, not a patch *owner*. A patch holder will guard his "colors" and defend them with his life, which is why there is a lot of respect shown to patch holders. Riding clubs have very few events they are required to attend. Motorcycle clubs must spend a lot of time at club events, their own, and of the neighboring MC's, primarily to show support for each other.

All clubs must show respect to each member, including prospects of clubs. Prospects are just that – living through a period of time where they *and* the club are both discerning whether their membership would be right for the club. It takes time to get to know who your new "relatives" will be and it is necessary to be certain that it is a family you really want to join.

Enjoy the "colors" you meet!

~

* THE KINDNESS OF STRANGERS *

~

Standing in line with my son one day at the local Barnes and Noble book store, waiting to pay for his Star Wars book, I noticed a man in front of me and a soldier behind me, both holding the books they were about to purchase. Suddenly the man in front of me looked up, noticed the soldier, excused himself while he walked in front of me and said "Soldier, let me buy that book for you." The soldier said, "Oh no, I got it…" The man said, "No, *I* got it," and took the soldier's book to the counter and paid for it along with his own. The soldier walked around and waited at the other end of the counter and when the man handed him the book, the soldier thanked him and introduced himself. The man shook his hand, said a few words, and then walked out the door, not waiting around for any kind of extra thanks and praise. My son looked at me and said, "That was nice!"

This encounter between those two men really made my day and just plain made me feel good. You don't see that stuff everyday. My friend, Carmella, owner of *New York Rider Magazine*, makes it a point to shake hands with every soldier she sees and thanks him/her for their service, sometimes going out of her way to do so. It's not unusual for bikers to offer help or show their support for different people or causes. These small gestures of kindness go a long way and are so easy to offer. I asked my son as we were leaving the store if he knew why the man bought the soldier's book. He said, "Yes, because maybe the soldier risked his life for him and he wanted to pay him back." Amazing, the wisdom of children. I have no doubt that witnessing the exchange between civilian and soldier made a difference, however small, in the lives of every person who was in line with us as well as the clerks behind the registers. It also brought to mind a well-known quote from the Bible: "Be not forgetful to entertain strangers, for thereby some have entertained angels unaware." **The only question is which one was the angel?**

~

DINO PETROCELLI
* Photographer *

"I have always put 110 percent into everything I do and have ever done - work, home, parenting, friendships."

Dino and I met in our early 20's. He was a photographer, then only as a hobby, and working in his family's sub shop. Dino always knew his place was behind the camera lens. His father gave him his first camera as a Christmas gift at the age of 14 and there was something about that little treasure that held Dino captivated. Dino couldn't seem to set the camera down for long and would bring it along with him to rock concerts, but he was not impressed with the quality of the pictures that were developed. This led him to his first 35mm camera and after a few years of shooting with the 35mm, Dino decided to try his hand at processing his own film, starting with black and white film and eventually adding color processing. Dino would often shoot pictures for the local bands and deliver 8x10 glossies to the band the following night. This impressed all the band members since back in the mid-1970's, having an 8x10 print developed the day following a photo shoot was unheard of (there were no one-hour photo labs back then).

Dino's photo career took a back seat while he served in the Navy on the aircraft carrier, Nimitz, from 1978 to 1981, working on F-14 Tomcats. Once Dino's military service was completed, his focus was back to photography.

Dino photographed his first wedding in 1985 for a friend, and his career was begun. In 1987, Dino started a small wedding business in Albany, New York, which is when he started to make money with the camera. The gift he received many years earlier had now become a money-making tool. After ten years of photographing weddings, Dino decided to expand into other areas, focusing on studio photography, learning all he could by experimenting with his own lighting techniques, and a lot of trial and error. Dino soon found himself working for independent companies and small ad agencies, photographing everything from gloves to car parts, operating rooms, and CD covers. Then, in 1997, Bikers Choice, a local motorcycle distributor, hired Dino to shoot the cover of their 1997 catalog. This would be Dino's first 'taste' of the motorcycle industry and before too long, he felt he found a new home shooting beautiful "iron horses," seeing through the camera lens the chrome, the paint, and the various designs on the bikes. Since then Dino has photographed for top national motorcycle magazines and the Discovery Channel. Dino's clients include: Discovery Channel, Orange County Choppers, Atlantic British Ltd., GMP Advertising, Swany Gloves, Grando Gloves, Ambrosino Designs, WTEN-TV, Bikers Choice, Kaiser Illustration, FLY92 and WPYX106 radio stations. Dino's work has appeared on many area billboards, CD covers, Barnett's Magazine, Hot Bike magazine, Easyriders Magazine, American Iron Magazine, Iron Horse, New York Rider Magazine, and numerous brochures and catalogs.

~

"I'm a professional photographer. I have been playing with cameras since I was 16, and it's been my only source of income for the past 15 years."

Dino tries to create an informal, comfortable environment and make all photo sessions enjoyable for everyone involved. His work can be very diverse, from documenting real surgeries in the operating room of a hospital, to product shoots for Atlantic British, a company that specializes in auto parts for Land Rover/ Range Rover. When the director of a hospital tells him he has only 30 minutes to go into the NICU and capture a shot of a mother, daughter and a premature baby, he does not have time to set up a myriad of lights. Clients appreciate the fact that Dino arrives with minimal equipment and gets the job done. He has a set of Calumet travel lights when he needs the power but most of the time he uses a Metz, which an assistant handles, and a Canon 550ex flash which is usually powered down one to two stops. The lighting he gets is amazing and appears as if he had used four or five lights. Not every shot is simple, though, but the challenges are why after 20 years Dino still loves what he does.

Dino keeps his motorcycle shoots simple and fun. The first thing he does is turn on the music with his surround-sound stereo system, power the 8x20-foot home-made light bank, loaded with four Calumet Elite flash heads, powered by two 2400-watt second Elite power packs with two heads in each back. The power packs hang from the rafters, one on each side of the light bank. Dino uses pocket wizards to avoid tripping over cords during the shoot. Many photographers have visited his studio and are amazed at the red, white and black color scheme of the studio (his logo colors). Dino makes the bike come alive through lighting, lens choice and angles, and his own artistic creativity. These are the photos you see on the Discovery Channel website and in many publications. Dino has photographed every OCC theme bike, including the "Old-School" series which can be found in the Barnett's OCC collection edition.

Dino's equipment includes a Canon Mark II, and a 10D as a backup (to upgrade soon). Lenses are 15mm, 70-200 2.8is, 85 1.2, 24-70, 50 1.4, 15-35 2.8- 2 24000 watt power packs with five heads, three travel light 750's, Canon 550, and two Metz 60ct4 flash heads. Dino uses a G4 Power book for location, and a G4 tower in the studio, with a 20-inch screen. His primary software programs are Photoshop CS and Extensis 6 to keep files in order. Dino's studio is 45x65x18 and he has recently photographed several cars in the new studio.

Dino designed his studio to be a place where he and his clients would be comfortable and still convey a professional atmosphere, with a lot of his work on display. To quote Dino, "Photography for me is not solely about making money. I have a beautiful family and a beautiful studio and at age 52, I am enjoying my life now more than ever. I have always maintained an 'open-door policy,' and other photographers are welcome to sit in on a shoot or ask questions."

~

"Life can be scary, never knowing what's around the next corner. It scares me to think my kids have to go through life and witness all the bad things in the world. All you can do is hope they make the right decisions and choose the right path. I'll always be afraid for the safety of my kids till the day I die."

Dino and I have three children, Sara, Sophia, and Dino Jr., who have been the center of our lives since the day they were born. Dino is a wonderful, loving father, devoted to his children, and always there for them, no matter what he may be involved with. He has never turned his back on his kids, even when he's been pushed to the limit of his patience (and that would have been an easy way out). He has always been committed to his family and never wavers in his responsibilities to them. Dino makes time for family and friends, in fact, more often he forgets to make time for himself and at times must be forced to take a break and REST.

Dino is a wonderful husband and a great provider, very often working 12-15 hour days and weekends, which has enabled me to keep a part-time job and be home for the kids when they needed me. He is a hero to our children and loves to be a kid along with them when the mood strikes, with a wicked sense of humor and the ability to laugh at himself and his own silly antics.

~

"The most defining time of my life was joining the military. I graduated high school and one week later I was in boot camp. That took me from boyhood to adulthood very fast. It helped me at a young age to make decisions on my own and it gave me great responsibility and leadership in my life. It's made me a better man, father, and husband. I believe everyone should have to enlist at least one term in the military. I think the world would be a better place."

Dino grew up in Castleton, New York, with his parents, Dominick and Faith, and two brothers, well-known local musician, Rocky Petrocelli, and the youngest brother, Paulie.

His father was very strict with him, perhaps because he was the middle child. His older brother was focused on his future career and his younger brother was born deaf and naturally given more attention. There was a lot of love in his home, but his father was determined to mold his children the way he felt was best for them. His father basically forced him into joining the Navy and at 19, Dino found himself, somewhat reluctantly, being sent to boot camp at the Great Lakes Naval Station in Illinois, and eventually serving at sea on the USS Nimitz, stationed in Virginia Beach for three years. Although Dino resented his parents for allowing him to be sent so far from his family and friends, he later appreciated the experience and understood the wisdom of his father's decision at that time. Today, Dino enjoys reconnecting with Navy buddies and loves to reminisce.

~

"I was working the night shift on the USS Nimitz and because I was getting discharged in two weeks, they switched me to days. The day after they switched me, there was a horrific plane crash on the deck at night, and one of the guys who died was doing the job that I would have been doing."

Dino has a compassionate heart and will do everything in his power to work for a cause he believes in. There is nothing he wouldn't do for a friend in need, and this, in addition to his ties to local businesses and charities, has earned him the greatest respect from his colleagues in the photography business as well as his peers in the biker community. If Dino is involved with a charity run or a photo exhibit, you can be sure a large crowd is guaranteed.

~

"I don't judge people. People make their own decisions. If I don't like the decisions my friends make, I distance myself from them. I do surround myself with happy, positive people. I think the friends I choose are a good mix. In school, I would hang around with 'heads' and 'jocks'. Today, I have friends in bike clubs, and not in bike clubs, I have friends that are 'heads' and 'jocks' and friends that are gay and straight. The bottom line to me is never judge if you don't want to be judged. I like the life

I chose and I would not change a thing, except maybe to invest more money at a younger age."

Dino's friends come from all walks of life. The way you look and how much money you make means nothing to him. Dino's best friend could be a millionaire or the homeless man living on the streets. He judges only the inside of a person and he believes in second chances. He knows how to forgive and forget and will work to keep a friendship, old or new. Dino will be the one to reach out to a friend who has drifted and try to reconnect. His father was a very sociable man, frequently striking up conversations with strangers and as a result collecting friends wherever he roamed. Dino takes after his father in that respect. If he can say or do something to brighten someone's day, he will. He is a compassionate man who seems to feel the pain of others and suffer along with them. There were times in my life when I was suffering and I don't know what I would have done without his constant love and support. He is a good, generous man, and never asks for anything in return.

~

"I was a teenager when I rode the first time - a mini bike and then a dirt bike. Then my father sold the dirt bike out from under me to my cousin Ronnie and I never rode again till the age of 39. I started shooting for a motorcycle parts company and seeing all the cool bikes finally convinced me that I had to tell the wife I needed to buy a bike. I took the safety course in 1998 and never looked back."

One of the most life-changing events in our lives was the day Dino bought his first motorcycle. It was a black Honda Sabre and his plan was to ride it "for practice" around the neighborhood until he gained more experience on the bike. He figured he'd keep the Sabre a few years, and then have a custom built exactly the way he wanted. It turned out he only kept the bike for a year before he commissioned someone to start building his dream bike. The finished product was a baddass custom with a Buell engine, painted black at first, then as time went on, two or three different paint themes. The only problem with the bike was that it was not made to handle a passenger and I was getting more and more anxious to ride on the back with him. Finally, when the time was right, Dino bought a Harley-Davidson Road King but kept the custom for his "boy's night out" rides, and our journey into the biker world had begun.

~

"Riding to me is riding, I feel more alive, I feel happy, I clear my mind, I love the smells, I love the hot and cold pockets you feel, but I don't think of it as a spiritual thing for me. It's just a release of all the pressures you have in life."

Dino became involved with *New York Rider Magazine* when Carmella Brown, the owner, called to ask if he'd be willing to shoot some photos for her magazine, still new at the time, and if he might think about advertising in the magazine. Dino of course was interested and thus began our relationship with Carmella and everyone involved with *New York Rider*. We were all committed to getting it off the ground and looked forward to watching it grow, from its roots in Syracuse, to all other areas of New York State. Since I love writing, I started contributing articles and when Carmella lost her Editor, I voluntarily assumed that position. Since then a whole new world was opened up to me. Dino is now the chief photographer for *New York Rider* and I am still the Editor. Our collaboration was the perfect combination for both of us. We are able to work together and we take pride in contributing to the success of the magazine.

~

"I regret not having a better relationship with my father in my later years and I wish I had started my photography career sooner."

Dino's only regret is that he and his father were not able in later years to establish a close relationship. His father was a stubborn man and at times was very difficult to reason with. To avoid more conflict, Dino would choose to end disagreements and not continue the fight, so the distance would become greater. Dino's father died at age 63. If they had more time, perhaps their relationship would have mended, but life is unpredictable and the most important factor was that Dino knew his father loved him.

~

"I would love to travel cross country, by car if necessary,
but I really want to do it on my bike.
That is on my bucket list."

Dino does not call himself a biker, rather, he is a photographer who rides a motorcycle. His life revolves around family and photography and he has built his career from the "ground up," teaching himself all the tools of the photography trade, learning primarily by experience. Presently, he is one of the master photographers in the Capital Region, a success he can call his own, and he will leave a legacy for which his family will forever be proud.

~

"Do unto others as you would have them do unto you."

DINO PETROCELLI

* FALLING IN LOVE
WITH A BIKER *

~

Loving a biker is not for the faint of heart. There will be more passion and probably more pain. Feelings will be intense and will consume your mind. You will have great difficulty concentrating and might be incapable of making any logical decisions. Sounds like normal, everyday, mushy love-at-first-sight stuff, doesn't it? The difference with bikers is the instinctive anxiety mixed with the passion, which adds volatility.

Every time your man (or woman) walks out the door, that little twinge of apprehension rears its head again. You hug a little tighter, a little closer; knowing that each time he hops on the bike, there is potential danger. You play this continuous game of jeopardy even though every hug could be the last. However, there will be no attempt to stop him because your efforts would be futile. The same reasons that cause you concern are the reasons you fell in love in the first place. He is a man of convictions and is true to his word. He is willing to take risks. Bikers are driven by excitement and challenges.

With every ride you take, you collect another friend and your circle grows wider. Your only rival for attention may be his bike. The bike is another best friend, to be cared for and respected. Bikers have bigger hearts because they're usually holding more in those hearts. They hold the love of their family and friends, the gratitude toward the brother who helped him when he was down, the sister he comforted when she lost her man, the people he has bonded with through years on the road, the constant sense of trepidation that is so worth the gamble, and YOU. These qualities altogether make for a powerful relationship, whether as friends or lovers. Everything a biker does is done with a stronger zeal. Call him wild, crazy, sometimes hazardous and extreme; he deserves every title.

Yours truly falls in love with bikers every day. My own heart, a former lightweight, has grown heavy with devotion...and it is divine.

~

* VIEW FROM THE
BACK SEAT *

~

The world looks very different from the seat of a motorcycle. We went for a long ride on a recent Sunday in September, 300 miles round trip (this ride was not for the Prima Donnas). The group we were with really love to ride, not stop every half hour. We set out around 9:00 AM with about 40 other bikes. I had no idea where we were going. I just wanted to ride on the bike and hopefully see some Fall foliage. We rode from Albany, New York, to Old Forge.

We started out and were soon passing through the first town, Schenectady, then on to Ballston Spa, Fort Plain, and very rural Herkimer! I am thinking, how *do* those hay bales get rolled anyway? Oh, there's another town sign, now we're in Poland. It smells nice around here and the trees are starting to look very colorful, almost psychedelic. We're approaching some winding roads and my husband is doing just fine with his new ape hangers. I'm noticing all kinds of things I never noticed before while riding through these towns, one being that just 30 minutes outside of Albany looks like the Amish Country with farms as far as the eye can see!

Then there are the cows grazing out in the fields. What do cows do for fun anyway? Here comes another town sign – Canajoharie, and there's the Beechnut factory we always see when we're traveling on the thruway, only now it's right around the corner. It's so cute how the old ladies take pictures of the bikers as we pass by and the little boys stand next to their fathers with that look of envy in their eyes, hoping their dad will notice how much they are admiring the motorcycles and take note of that for future reference. Passing through a few more towns, we finally reach our destination of Old Forge, New York, and start looking for a place to eat. We ended up at a small place on Route 28 which didn't need a menu since all they served was hamburgers or cheeseburgers! There were nine of us, and most of us ordered cheeseburgers and sodas. The bill was just $18 (for all nine of us!) The burgers were tasty and the people were friendly, and all for less than what you'd pay at McDonalds! We headed home after eating but took a different route and rode through Long Lake, North Creek, Lake George, Glens Falls and Saratoga, and ended our trip at a BBQ on Western Avenue in Guilderland, New York. A great day spent with some great people.

Dino and I took another day trip in October, this time with a smaller crowd, but a trip just as beautiful. We were all supposed to meet at a friend's house and we arrived to find only two other guys there ready to roll. I didn't mind being the only female (sometimes it's more fun). We followed our leader along some winding roads through Columbia County. The Fall foliage was even more brilliant this time, almost a month later than our last ride. Perhaps we've passed this way before in the car with the kids, but I definitely don't remember seeing the mountains I saw this time. Riding on a few of the roads felt like walking through a painting depicting a perfect Autumn path leading to wherever. I realize how lucky we are to live in this charming, picturesque State of New York. Passing through Egremont and Great Barrington, Massachusetts, after riding about 60 miles, we found ourselves in Canaan, Connecticut! We came to a clearing at what seemed like the top of a mountain and stopped to snap a few pictures. We could see mountains in the distance, the colors a vibrant red, orange, yellow, green, and a valley with a lake at the bottom. We parked the bikes in a spot worthy of the view and captured the moment with our cameras.

This time we ate at a roadside café and enjoyed some sandwiches and drinks. Riding home, I strained my neck trying to eyeball all the antiques we passed. Connecticut must be notorious for them! We passed a few farms along the way and I wondered what it would be like to live on one and be sharing my days with cows and crops, and of course those hay bales.

I took a weekend trip to Texas and was amazed at the terrain of the earth flying from Chicago down to Dallas. For at least an hour all I saw were square patches of land – dark brown, beige, rust, green – absolutely amazing. Riding on the motorcycle reminds me of that feeling I had when I was in the plane looking out the window. Everyone should experience the view from a plane and from a motorcycle. The big difference is that from a plane you are really just an observer; from a motorcycle you become *part* of the earth! The smells are more pronounced, the trees are so close that you can actually distinguish their scent, you appreciate the perfume of the flowers you see, and you can't believe how many different porches you pass. You start to relate to what it's like to be a small creature in the woods or a butterfly or a bug and you wish you could freeze days like this and re-live them whenever the mood strikes. Life is beautiful on a bike!

~

EDDIE
* Turbulent *

"What you represent belongs to you – Loyalty, Honor, Respect, and Brotherhood."

Eddie's reputation preceded him, so I met him with a somewhat preconceived opinion in my mind of the kind of man he was. Eddie was tried and found innocent of a crime at which he acted in self-defense and I believed everything the media spoon-fed to us about this man. However, I did become aware of Eddie's potential innocence through the media work of Hank McGrath and the Spirit of Biker Brotherhood documentaries on TV, and came to know its truth when I actually met him in person. He was charming, very welcoming, and I felt almost instantly that I was shaking hands with a good man. Yes, he may be impulsive, may have dangerous faults, but somehow I knew that he had a good heart.

I recall a story told to me about how Eddie, who lived in the Bronx as a youth, protected a frail, defenseless kid on the block from bullies. It's not that he took a liking to the kid. He just did not like defenseless people being victimized by creeps and bullies. As the story goes, years later Eddie sees this same kid, now a grown man, in the neighborhood with a new high-class car and two females holding each arm, flaunting himself. It seems this fellow became a big movie star and as Eddie approached him to give his greeting and respect the guy said to

Eddie, "Hey, run over to the store and get us some sodas, will you?," as if Eddie were a chump! Eddie, of course, told him "No" (and probably a few more expletives), turned around and walked away, leaving the guy in shock and shame. It has been pretty much like that for Eddie – standing up for those who later have no worthy appreciation for his help. But that does not stop his good character.

~

"I was 10 years old when I rode a Motocross bike. I was 15 when I rode my first motorcycle (with no license). I was 18 years old when I had my first Harley, which I built myself out of spare parts from a 1959 Panhead."

Eddie is 48-years-old and started riding bikes at a very early age and has never been without a motorcycle, since owning his first Harley at 18 years old. His interest in bikes has never wavered and always remained a priority in his life, even when logic would have dictated that he focus on more important things.

~

"I see myself as a free spirit."

He loves life on the road, so chose a career of driving a tractor trailer, which may be one of the reasons Eddie never married and so far has no children. However, this man has had many relationships *("I've been in love a handful of times")* but has yet to find his soul mate. I know Eddie has a huge cache of friends, male and female, which is attributable to his warm personality and willingness to accept anyone into his life who will not hold judgment against him. There is still too much pre-judging in the world. This is an extremely valuable lesson that I learned myself from my association with Eddie and all of the members of his club.

~

"The things that scare me are heights and the thought of being buried alive. I have recurring dreams of being buried alive."

I wonder why Eddie dreams of being buried alive. Hank, who has become a close friend of Eddie's, suggests that this has to do with the unseen future, power of nature and fate. So many misjudgments have been placed upon this man that he fears being unjustly accused again and "buried alive" by it all. He searches for total peace. Eddie states that he believes in God. If he nurtures that faith, God will see him through the residual pain and he will someday finally find true contentment. Eddie is a rebel and a free spirit, but he takes the time to feel the heart of his conscience, a conscience filled with sadness for the loss of life for which others caused him to be involved.

~

"I judge the people I surround myself with by how truthful and down-to-earth they are. I admire people who don't think they are better than anyone else, or have attitudes."

Eddie values the truth and expects honesty and loyalty from his friends. He prefers to be around those who are "straight shooters," who do not put on airs or preface every encounter with an attitude. Eddie has no tolerance for conceit, which is probably why he is always surrounded by people who share this opinion. He has always been a defender of those who are helpless and tells me he "can't stand bullies!" He told me a story about living in the Bronx and witnessing a guy mug an old woman. Eddie ran after the mugger and beat him up (after the guy shot Eddie). The cops finally showed up and the newspapers the next day touted the incident as "Bikers to the Rescue!" Right is right and wrong is wrong. Most people are comfortable around Eddie because of his unpretentious manner and ready smile. In fact, it may take longer for Eddie to be at ease with others but that is a natural response from someone whose trust does not come quickly. However, once the barrier is broken with Eddie, you have a friend for life.

~

"I have a few regrets - not staying in school, not joining the military, and a few unmentionable things that I have done. Because of my mistakes, I struggle with my own demons on a daily basis."

As time passed and I spent more time around Eddie and learned more about him, I found that my instincts were correct. He is no angel but neither is he full of evil. Instead, he is the "club comedian," constantly pulling pranks and telling jokes. Eddie is often the life of the party at events! Eddie is loyal and honorable to his word. He's always doing things for the community, for example, giving candy out to local neighborhood kids near the clubhouse. The kids can be seen running up to him like he is "The Godfather!" He is not discriminatory and would help people struggling through hardship and troubles, regardless of who they are (with the exception of child abusers). He is actually an excellent ambassador for the public, representing a real one-percenter. Another example is Eddie's care of his friend, Supe, who was homeless and struggling in family court. Eddie helped Supe relocate and took care of him until his recent untimely death. Hank enlisted Eddie as the Godfather of his daughter, AlannaWillow, solely because, as Hank says, "Later on, after I am gone, I *know* he would forever assist her with anything she needed."

Eddie at one time owned a hot dog and burger place in Watervliet. He also owned his own truck. He had to close the business and sell the truck to survive when he was released from jail with no funds. He has still not recovered from the deceit, backstabbing, and losses he suffered when he was falsely accused. He learned that whether a person is innocent or not means nothing to the attorneys since all they want is a conviction. Surprisingly, Eddie harbors no ill will toward cops. *"If we didn't have laws, we'd be living in a 'Mad Max' world."* As he said to me, *"A job is a job and I respect people who work, no matter what they do."* However, he *does* stand against the harassment of bikers by law enforcement.

~

"I hung around with clubs in NYC all my life. I relocated to the Capital District and ran into an old friend who was part of a club and after spending time with him, I decided to join so I would have the brotherhood and loyalty of a club. The club is the only family I have and I am very close to them."

Eddie is a member of the 69ers Motorcycle Club North Country Crew from Troy, New York. Most men who join motorcycle clubs join for a reason and very often the reason involves a search for something that is absent in their life. Eddie has sisters and his father is still alive but he is not close to his family, although he did see his mother from time to time until her recent death. Eddie freely admits he's made a lot of mistakes and does not blame his parents for his behavior. He is a product of his environment (says he can't help it that he always wanted to grow up and be a "gangster" like the ones he would see in the movies). For Eddie, his natural need was for the closeness of a family, a family he could spend time with, rely on and love unconditionally. Eddie was not raised within a traditional, conventional family, and joining the club provided him with the missing "branches" on his family tree. His brothers stood by him and supported him during his darkest days and have proven their loyalty beyond a doubt. Eddie will forever be grateful for the unceasing love and support of the 69ers MC.

~

"I did not graduate from high school or college. I believe wisdom comes from a combination of age, experience and suffering. You learn a little from each over the years."

It is said there are two types of intelligence on this planet: book smart and street smart. Eddie is the latter and no less clever or intelligent than a man with a college degree. We know there are some things that cannot be learned from a textbook. The most important life lessons are impossible to learn without experiencing pain and pleasure firsthand and acquiring the wisdom which comes from conquering adversity.

~

"I have been close to death a few times. I have been beaten into a coma, I have been shot. It's just a wild lifestyle. It all comes with a lifestyle of growing up in the Bronx in the early 1980's."

Anyone who faces serious illness or death experiences a certain revelation. Your mortality becomes crystal clear and you become conscious of how small you really are. You see yourself as just another star in the galaxy, but then you realize how significant your life has been and how dark the sky would be if every star had fallen. The experience changes your perspective and causes you to see your life and those around you through different eyes – wise eyes. Many find much more to be grateful for after "dancing with the Devil." Have these incidents made Eddie the "cautiously crazy" character he is today?

~

"My favorite movie of all time is 'Casino'."

Eddie spends a lot of time gambling with his life! His decisions are a gamble in the present state of things, while he rebuilds his life after unjustly losing everything he owned.

~

"Riding helps to clear my mind and helps to put me at ease."

Eddie grew up in the Bronx and moved here when he was 32. The freedom of riding a motorcycle was the perfect escape from the noise and chaos of the city. Now, Eddie needs the bike to relax. His motorcycle is a comfort to him when stress takes over. Eddie loves to ride the open highways, sometimes to air out his soul, and, as the 69ers always say, "ride with the pack and give something back." The 69ers MC relate themselves with the wolf.

Ironically, Eddie wishes to record his life in print and I know he has a fascinating story to tell. Perhaps this chapter will serve as a catapult for his own autobiography. My impression of Eddie, based on my own interactions with him, is of a caring, compassionate man, a strong champion of "underdogs," and a faithful friend. I am proud to be counted as one of his.

~

"You can do a thousand good deeds but fuck up once and NO ONE forgets."

{Eddie dedicates this chapter to his friend & brother, the late Big John "Supe" Supinaw, of South Troy}

EDDIE

* TIME TO MEET THE OUTLAWS *

~

It is fascinating that the outlaw club subculture can exist and actually thrive in today's society. There is a lesson here. If you understand the brotherhood aspect inherent and maybe mandatory, in clubs, you eventually see the relationship to a family structure that the brotherhood nurtures, and thus why this subculture succeeds.

Consider the 'class' structure of an outlaw club: "Hangaround"; Prospect; Full patch member. There is good reason for this class structure. Just as in traditional families, there is a hierarchy – President Dad, Co-Pres Mom, and down (or up) the line (Polywog, Tadpole, Frog). In every society there are class structures and outlaw clubs are no different. Respect is a major factor here. The prospect must go through a process of discernment first to determine whether the club is the right fit for him and then to ensure that he learns and earns the respect that will be required of him as a full patch member. This process forces an evolution of the soul. Kind of like having to walk in someone's shoes before you really "get" it. You're young before you're old. Experience before wisdom. Darkness before dawn, you get the drift.

I admire the brotherhood ideal in these clubs. There is discipline, there is respect, and there is love. They are part of an elite group and are proud to represent each other. "Greater love has no one than this, that one lay down his life for his friends." This stuff doesn't just happen. Takes time and sacrifice, just like any lasting relationship in life.

Do we have family secrets or skeletons in our personal closets? Yes. Do we get justifiably provoked if one of the family members airs our dirty laundry or throws one of those skeletons out for all to see? Of course. Do we take action to preserve our dignity and respect? Yes. Are you noticing a pattern here? Family. Values. No question that outlaw clubs have been notorious for criminal behavior, even if they were not truly guilty of every accusation. But how different really are these guys from the average citizen you pass on the street every day? These are not super-human beings with supernatural powers. Most of us live insulated within our little cocoons, always careful not to step out of the cocoon and shed our skin. Perhaps one difference is they choose *not* to always hide their sins – and do shed that skin now and then. Maybe they actually enjoy being the rebel with or without a cause. Haven't we all felt that way at some time in our lives. If we walked around with our sins typed up and displayed on our chests, we would all be declared candidates for a ticket to Hell.

Families are continually struggling with generation gap issues, personality conflicts, disagreements among family members, faulty decision-making. What do families do when they are struggling? They may have a family meeting, they may turn to their faith for strength to get through the days and weeks, and they may even call on relatives. Club brothers behave in similar ways. Some attend meetings, called 'church,' in which various issues are discussed – financial, upcoming events, problems that need solutions. Working together, the club members find the resolutions they seek and business is taken care of. Occasionally, club members may call upon support clubs for assistance. Some clubs grow very close and the relationship is akin to that of cousins who are almost as close as brothers. The reference, "brother of a different patch" can be a high honor achieved over time. A full patch member is indeed a full member of the club and inherits all the benefits entitled to him, but earning the patch does not mean everyone in the club automatically gets along with each other, or always agrees. Personality conflicts are dealt with, individuals may compromise for the good of the club, and life goes on. Bottom line is whatever each member brings to the table is what makes a club what it is – just like with any family you are there for good times and bad.

Outlaw clubs have their own ancestors and I'm sure many of them actually trace that genealogy. Walk into a clubhouse if you ever have the opportunity, and notice all the "family" pictures on the walls. Also notice the care and reverence taken with their placement. These photos represent those from the club who have gone before them. Current members look to those ancestors as their heroes, their mentors, their soldiers who have paved the way for future generations of the dynasty. We learn from our ancestors, we learn our history and tradition and we carry it on.

We are loyal to our family and friends. Club members are loyal to each other, in fact, club members can probably count on their 'brothers" as much if not more than family members. This fact is well-known and one of the reasons that brothers are willing to sacrifice so much time and energy to their club. They know to whom they pledge their allegiance, and they are devoted to promoting the good of the club. Just as we might forfeit certain relationships in order to preserve the consistency of our family structure, the outlaw will place a high priority on his club brothers and may consider them first before his own family. This tells us how serious the brotherhood relationship is in this culture. If that relationship is severed, trust is breached, and there are usually serious consequences for the club and its offending member. Kind of like when Amish families 'shun' the male or female defector. They are never allowed back into the family and are no longer acknowledged, they become invisible. The club president must insure that no fracture results in a shattered foundation. Though a branch may be broken from the tree, the tree remains standing tall and continues to grow.

The promise of security is naturally appealing to potential prospects, especially (but not exclusively) to those who hail from broken families or damaged affairs of the heart and soul. Club brothers vow to protect, defend, and support each other at all costs. The initiation process is worth the reward that is earned. Another family member is born and the occasion is marked by celebration. Members are dedicated to contributing to the benefit of the club and partnership with neighboring coalitions. Their ambition is driven by a desire for acceptance and amity among each other and with neighboring outlaw clubs. While at first a member may appear guarded, it is simply his innate sense of potential danger. Only when a man earns his full patch does he finally feel at peace in the company of his brothers. All members are considered equal. Brothers greet each other with handshakes or hugs to stress the significance of the member's status and remunerate the brother for his loyalty and ambition.

I see the future of outlaw clubs much in the same way the family structure has evolved today. There are just as many divorced families as families who stay together. Those who stay together know they have to work through all the dynamics of their family empire, at every stage of their lives, whether living through great times or struggling through trying times. The way I see it, family and club life are closely intertwined and both possess the basic need to love, survive and prosper. And what remains, despite all odds, is the constant birth and continued growth – some laws of nature cannot be halted. The club family perseveres and the spirit of brotherhood is eternal.

~

RIDING WITH THE HELLS ANGELS

~

Riding with the Hells Angels is a rare occurrence for me, but will be remembered as one of the best times of my life. My opportunity to ride with the "outlaws" for a day came back in 2008 when my husband was asked to photograph some club members for a special project while they were near Caroga Lake, New York, for a club event. When riding with the Hells Angels, or any club for that matter, there is of course a protocol to follow as far as the order of the club members, officers, and other club representatives. Civilians (like us) or guests, naturally, are to ride behind the pack.

Once we were given the signal that the Angels were ready to saddle up and take off, we prepared to follow the line of bikes, which seemed to stretch as far as my eyes could see. Hearing the rumble of the bikes was enough to rev me up for what was to come and my adrenaline was already rushing at that point. We took off and found ourselves having to accelerate quickly to keep up with the pack. We were on what most would consider winding "country roads" and were a little apprehensive about being able to continue. Even though it was a little scary for me, I knew Dino could handle it and I was enjoying every minute. While thinking to myself, "holy sh— I'm actually riding with the Hells Angels," I was amazed at the perfect formation those men kept, while riding like bats out of HELL! I never had a more exhilarating ride in my life, or felt such a sense of freedom, as if during that ride all restrictions were abandoned. The Angels ride well and they ride hard and fast! No one wavered or broke off from the pack, all the guys separate but totally in sync, and rode together until safely arriving at our destination.

Hopping off the bike with my Cheshire cat grin, I know my husband had to be thinking "Wow, she enjoyed this just a little *too* much," but I could not contain my excitement. One of my lifelong dreams had just come to fruition and it was pure rapture!

~

ERNIE
* Pride *

"I've done a lot of things and traveled a lot of places and now I want to do them all over again on my motorcycle. It's the only time I get to sit and think with the rain cloud up above being the only worry I have. ALIVE is one way of describing how I feel when riding, the other word would be FREEDOM."

Ernie is a Nomad member of the Warlocks Motorcycle Club of Cocoa Beach, Florida, currently living in Massachusetts. Ernie and I met at a biker event in the month of January. I introduced myself after receiving an email from him to inform me of his chapter's first anniversary party which he was planning for that Summer. He was very friendly and respectful and I liked him immediately, even though we hardly had the chance to talk that day. We got to know each other a little better when Carmella and I attended his party that June, and had the opportunity to meet many of his Warlocks brothers from around the country. With so many police around that day, it almost felt like we were in a movie, especially with this large group of Warlocks, men and women, proudly displaying their colors.

"The night I became a Warlock was the night my family went from being just a few to a family of thousands, and it hasn't stopped growing since. Being a Warlock defines who I really am in life - a father, a brother, a son, a

mentor, a friend - and someone who can wear many hats.
Underneath it all I'm a trustworthy man and some think
I'm a pretty good one too."

~

I attend many biker events all year round and one of the
things I never forget is how I am treated by the club members
hosting the event. Ernie treated Carmella and I like "sisters" and
I will never forget that. He was personable to us right off the bat
and essentially gave us the freedom to interview any of the club
members that we chose to speak with, as well as photograph
those who had no objections. The food that day was awesome
too, by the way, another factor I always seem to remember. I
enjoyed spending time with everyone even though most lived far
from my hometown and I knew I probably wouldn't be seeing
these people again anytime soon.   Most traveled from down
South to be there, and *all*, as far as I know, rode their bikes.

"I was brought up around bikes my whole life, from riding
on the gas tank of my brother's RD70 at age four, to the
many Jap bikes I've owned and crashed!! I bought my own
bike at age 18 (Kawasaki Eliminator) and had to keep it
over my neighbor's house so my mom wouldn't see it."

~

Ernie, like his brother John, was exposed to the motorcycle
world at an early age, which explains his love for riding and the
security he feels as a member of a motorcycle club. I keep up with
Ernie's travels, and he is constantly on the road to somewhere.
If it's cold where Ernie is, he just hops on his bike and rides to
someplace warm. There are Warlocks in several southern states
and members are always welcome to visit each other, as time
allows. From what I've seen, Ernie makes a conscious effort to
stay in close touch with his Warlocks MC brothers.

~

"Alcohol was a problem for awhile, but anyone who drinks
has had a problem one time in their life. That's why we
drink, isn't it? I have no real addiction to any chemicals
right now and I know that can always change, but with the
support system I have with my Warlocks brothers, I can't
see anything being a problem. They have my back 25/8."

Ernie makes his living as a heavy equipment salesman *("I could sell ice to an Eskimo")*, has been married since 2002, and has three "angels, one heavenly and two earthly." Ernie's children are his greatest treasures, and he cherishes his time with them. I have not had the pleasure of meeting them, but the photos I've seen of Madisyn and Mason are stunning. They are absolutely beautiful children. Ernie is present at every special event in his children's lives and for anything that a child needs his father. Ernie's children adore their Daddy and relish his love and affection. Their pictures tell the story of their devotion for each other.

~

"The loss of my baby girl, Dakota, and the birth of my two other children, taught me that we are just renting space here on this planet, and when the landlord wants us gone....WE'RE GONE!! So I live each day as if it was my last." (Favorite quote: "He who is deaf, blind, and silent will live a hundred years in peace")

Who among us can even begin to imagine the pain of losing a child unless we've suffered the same? Ernie's wife recalls the day their daughter died: *"As the doctor put the ultrasound machine on my belly, he placed it right over Dakotas's heart and what came next were words that I never want to hear again in my life: 'I am sorry but there is no heart beat.' I made him check a second and third time. He had to be wrong; this was not happening I must be dreaming. The next thing I heard was Ernie screaming, "NO" at the top of his lungs, punching the chair as hard as one could and then he just dropped to his knees. To hear that your daughter had just died and to see your husband who was my rock fall apart was more than any woman could handle at one time. We were no longer safe."* Ernie will never "get over" that loss and will probably grieve for the rest of his life, but instead of wallowing in self-pity, he has channeled his energy into being the best father he could possibly be to his children. Anyone who knows Ernie learns quickly that his son and daughter are the true owners of his heart. He tells me that he fell in love three times in his life, each time one of his children was born.

"I love to be part of my children's every move through life!! I cherish each and every day that I'm with them. I KNOW WHAT IT'S LIKE TO LOSE ONE!! And that's the number one reason I don't take my kids for granted, like many parents do. I don't have many fears in life but one thing that does scare me is the thought of me outliving my children!! Fear is something you can overcome!!"

When tragedy strikes, it is natural to blame God and it is no surprise that Ernie claims no faith in God.

~

"If there was a God whom many speak of, he wouldn't have taken my first love from me, and if there is such a God, I can't wait to see him. I've got a lot of questions for him and he aint gonna' like them, trust me!!" (Favorite quote: "I shut my eyes so that I can see")

Ernie has a sense of humor which would rival any professional comedian. He makes me laugh almost every time I'm around him because I never know what quirky statement will come out of his mouth. This is one of the reasons that Ernie has so many friends. He laughs at himself and seems to know how to eliminate all the awkwardness that usually comes with a first meeting.

~

"I graduated in 1988 from Wilmington High School, hated every minute of it, but wish I was still there! If I knew then what I know now...ohhh, those poor girls. Just saying!!" (Favorite quote: "A man doesn't pay a hooker for sex; he's paying her to leave.")

Ernie's luck with the ladies in his life would be due to his charming demeanor throughout the years, and of course a father, as his first teacher, who taught him about respect. I suspect there may be many women who envy Ernie's wife, just for the deep devotion and protectiveness he displays as a family man. He counts "Outlaw Josey Wales," "Unforgiven," and "Pale Rider" as his favorite movies, declaring that *"Clint Eastwood is the coolest motherfucker this planet has ever seen."*

"I consider my father one of my best friends and my brother, John, is someone I live for each and every day. He is the reason I'm alive today. Back on February 10, 1971, he saved my life when our house caught on fire. The same fire took my mother and my other two brother's lives."

~

Ernie's brother, John, is the National President of the Warlocks Motorcycle Club, and though they live hundreds of miles from each other, they are closer than brothers who see each other on a daily basis. They share a bond which will never be severed by distance or outside influences. John is Ernie's hero, that title bestowed upon only one other person, their father. Following in their giant footsteps, Ernie has learned love, honor, and sacrifice from his family mentors, those lessons serving to eventually elevate him to a leadership position within the club. They have been his guiding lights through every darkness that has threatened to shadow his life. Their strength and support pierced holes into the thick black clouds that surrounded Ernie after the death of his mother, brothers, and later, his own child. Without them, his spirit too would have died. His only regret is not moving to Florida when he had the chance so that he could see his brothers more often.

~

"Back in 1989, I was a passenger in a car and we hit a pole going about 90 mph. I broke both ankles, six ribs, suffered a skull fracture (I have a drill hole on my forehead), and multiple internal injuries. From what I've been told, I was minutes from being pronounced dead!! I have suffered and survived which made me stronger, knowing I can and will survive just about anything. And, as I grow older, I get a lot wiser from my daily mistakes and from past experiences!" (Favorite quote: "Life is hard, but it's harder if you're stupid")

A man's character is measured not by the mistakes he's made, but by his response to those mistakes. Ernie freely admits his imperfections; however, he has taken every unfortunate incident and found some valuable lesson in the experience. To examine your faults and your own conscience and come away a wiser man is an admirable trait. Ernie is determined to succeed in whatever he tries, and will not succumb to defeat.

~

"I am a Warlock because of the brotherhood that I had witnessed over the years, especially when my daughter, Dakota, had passed. The outpouring of love I got from my club was extremely overwhelming which is why I stopped at nothing to become a Warlock. The reason I stay is the same reason I joined - the BROTHERHOOD. I went from having one brother (Big John) to having 1,000 brothers and they all have my back unconditionally!!"

In my experiences with the Warlocks Nation, I have witnessed the strong brotherhood of which Ernie speaks. When members congregate, they are a family in every sense. They live, love, eat and breathe together. They do not turn away from their brother's problems because it might be inconvenient, rather, they immerse themselves completely and step up with no hesitation to help resolve the issue at hand and restore the necessary peace. When a Warlock is cut, all the Warlocks bleed, and if the situation requires a national Warlocks MC "tourniquet," then so be it!

As a friend, Ernie is loyal and compassionate. I know this because on several occasions, with nothing to gain, he has defended me in a few of my 'literary' battles. He has also praised and encouraged me since the day we met, and his support has motivated me to continue pursuing my passion for writing about the motorcycle world. Ernie is a proud man and never fails to display that pride for his family and his club, and that is further confirmed by the respect and dedication he shows for his friends.

~

"If you're gonna' just STARE at me, all you're gonna' see is the cover to MY book!"

ERNIE

* SPARE PARTS FOR BROKEN HEARTS *

~

Maybe it's my imagination but the biker friends I have collected over the years have given me more pure pleasure and deeper pain than any others in my life up to this point. The justification for this is surely due, in part, to the fact that biker friendships are forged from a common denominator – sharing something we love – our love of riding. Senses are heightened by the automatic risk we all freely accept and the natural excitement that accompanies those emotions. Is it any wonder that with every successive ride the bond gets stronger? Bikers learn how fleeting life is, maybe brutally so. Despite our best efforts to prevent accidents, they continue to plague the biker community. We lose one of our own, however we lose them, or we hear of a friend going down, and we all feel the pain. My guess is most bikers will immediately think to themselves, "There but for the grace of God go I."

The anguish is very close to the pain and anxiety of ending a relationship and losing someone you love. Thoughts of your loss pervade your mind and the tears flow involuntarily. The world changes in some way and your heart is broken.

It is no secret that bikers seem to enjoy a love affair with their bikes and will handle their precious machines almost as they would a child. Still, bikers cherish their friends even more. That kind of love is intense, passionate and irreplaceable. A motorcycle can be fixed or replaced but the loss of a member from our circle is felt indefinitely. The grief continues until the pain subsides.

If only there were spare parts for broken hearts.

~

* THERE GOES THE NEIGHBORHOOD *

~

It is disheartening to hear people preach on subjects they know nothing about but believe they are somehow an authority nevertheless. Where is this more prominent than in the biker world? Bikers suffer from discrimination, just as any other "culture," yet that discrimination is ignored or considered justified.

When a pack of bikers ride together, there will be crowds lined up on both sides of the street just to watch them. It's amazing that bikers will bring the woman out of the house who only minutes before finished putting rollers in her hair. If there are children nearby, they will race each other to the end of the driveway just for a chance to wave at the bikers. Grandma and Grandpa will stroll on out for a glimpse of the crowd. Recently, while riding in a pack, there on one of the street corners stood a woman with bright red hair, professionally dressed, waving at us as we rode by, both of her arms flailing wildly. You never know who or what you will see on the road. What is it that makes people so fascinated with bikers? And why do some of those same people stomp on their rights?

Often, when bikers pass through your neighborhood, they are riding in honor of a friend, or participating in a charity ride for someone or something to which they feel compelled to contribute, or simply minding their own business and riding for the hell of it. Yet, there are those who will hide behind their curtains and follow the bikers' every move, criticizing their lifestyle while putting on the guise that they don't want anything to do with them, but in certain circles at convenient times are quick to announce, "Oh yeah, I know a one-percenter, my cousin's boyfriend's friend is a Hells Angel."

This blatant discrimination was made crystal clear recently in the case of the Sons of Sam Motorcycle Club (a veterans club) in Syracuse, New York, who were denied an application by the Geddes Zoning Board because they would cause an "adverse affect on the environment" (a zoned area which has a bar with motorcycle-riding patrons operating several doors down). One has to wonder if we would see the same result had it been a minority group applying. No doubt a racism war would ensue.

Time to learn more about the biker culture and look a little closer at what is at stake here. Take away the rights of bikers and watch how fast your own freedom is restricted. No more cheap thrills watching the bikers pass by, instead you'll be renting movies (if that's allowed), such as Easy Rider or Wild Hogs, to learn what a "biker" was.

~

PATRICK MURPHY AKA FOURSPEED
* Courage *

"I'm a good person that you can take or leave. I don't tend to sell myself to others. I just am."

This will be one of the most difficult chapters for me to write because I have never met FourSpeed in person, and there will always be that insight missing – the insight I would have felt upon meeting him face to face. However, since FourSpeed lives in Texas and I in New York, our paths do not cross, and despite the distance, it was very important for me to include him in this book, as he has had a significant impact on my life.

I met FourSpeed online back around 1998, about the same time I acquired a home computer and email address. I was learning my way around the internet and my husband was planning to buy his first motorcycle, and one day asked me, since I was on the computer, to start searching for some information on bikes. While surfing and searching for all things motorcycles, I somehow stumbled upon a website called VBMO, short for Virtual Biker Motorcycle Organization. I started to read through the site and found there was some useful technical information as well as a message board. Figuring I had nothing to lose and could maybe learn something, I decided to join the discussions. It was not a particularly welcoming experience, and someone else may have backed away immediately, however, I found the characters intriguing at first glance, and knew there had to be a lot more to these people than met my eye at that moment. I was definitely treated as a "newbie" (maybe more like a prospect) and some put me to the test as far as where I came from, why I was there and what the hell did I know about motorcycles. Confessing that I knew next to nothing, only that my husband was building a custom, and I hoped to be riding with him soon, I started to get replies from a few, accusing us of being RUB's (rich urban bikers), yuppies, or posers. Even though I was not a jaded motorcyclist, I knew what those words meant and could not understand why these people were insulting me right off the bat. After a few more similar posts, I was almost ready to throw in the mouse, until this guy named FourSpeed appeared on the forum. He quickly realized what was happening and said something, in a matter-of-fact way, which seemed to "put them (the forum members) in their place." Obviously this man was somebody important because after that incident, everyone seemed to heed his words and be a little friendlier toward me.

~

"As for judging people, well, I'm not really into judging others. They are what they are, who am I to say how they should live their lives? There are many that make me sad with their choices but life is about choices, be they good or bad. I can't abide bullies, be they kids or adults, and I've seen my share of them all my life. So perhaps I do a bit of judging since I can't stand bullies or people with children that don't realize just how precious they are."

FourSpeed was in fact the President of the VBMO at the time and I was not surprised to learn that. I have never forgotten that small act of compassion he showed toward me, even though he knew absolutely nothing about this new "Lisa" on the forum, and as far as I was concerned, his actions from that day forward revealed a wise, judicious, and honorable man, who I am proud to call a friend, one of the treasured "people in my computer."

FourSpeed explained to me, in his own, friendlier way, that the members were good people but they all believed that anyone who enters their world should spend time becoming familiar with the place before jumping in, sort of like knocking before you open the door and step in. He told me to hang in there and get used to the people posting messages, try to learn who was who, and that once they all realized that I was not a threat in any way they would share more of themselves with me. He was right. I think the greatest lesson I learned about bikers from my experience at the VBMO was the vast differences in temperament among the biker culture and that you never really know where someone is coming from or what is happening in their life which could be affecting their judgment. Patience is another quality that comes to mind when I think about FourSpeed. He always seemed to consider all the angles in a given situation, and to me his comments always made sense.

Anxious to learn more about this man, FourSpeed, I browsed through his own website, Murphy's Law, and was able to see several photos of his family, though hardly any of himself, something that stayed in the back of my mind. I learned that he was married to a beautiful woman named Donita and from what I could tell from the photographs, he always seemed to be surrounded by children. I don't recall asking him too many questions about his family life but I could sense there was some sadness mixed in with the joyful images I saw in the photos.

~

"I remember learning that all parents aren't heartless bastards, and going to Vietnam as a kid and seeing firsthand how stupid and cruel humans can be. Both made me a better human being who doesn't take anything for granted. I've built a lot of walls around me over the years and not many are allowed within. Just is."

I figured there must be too much pain there and it was not my business or my right to know about any of it. You would assume that someone who has suffered in their past would tend to project that onto everyone they meet. This is not the case with FourSpeed. Whatever his cross, he carries it well, and no doubt his trials have only served to make him a humble, hard-working, intelligent man with some strong principles, who is greatly admired by all who know him. I don't need to know everything about him to know that is true. "He just is."

FourSpeed has been a biker just about all of his life, having ridden his first motorcycle *"with my dad when I was five or six, on my own bike when I was ten, and never looked back from there."* He knows motorcycles, wrenches on his own bike and has taught his children to do the same.

~

"Other kids were putting cards in their spokes and I was riding my own motorcycle to school. You can't get away with that kind of stuff anymore. We're turning the nation into a bunch of sissies. The country is geared toward the weakest link instead of the strongest.
It's sad what we're becoming."

FourSpeed is an extremely intelligent, well-read man who has opinions on every topic under the sun, including politics and religion. He talks of our country's values being stripped one by one and longs to see changes for the sake of his children and grandchildren. He does not take a careless attitude about the future. *"I've been married 40 years, have two kids and six grandkids. My son lives close by me but my daughter lives in my old stomping grounds in California."*

FourSpeed's description of himself as a father was in keeping with my perception of him – a devoted family man who is non-judgmental and never too proud to admit his mistakes. I have actually had the chance to speak online with his daughter, Tammy (aka Sassy), a few times and it was obvious how much she loves and adores her father. What a wonderful legacy he will leave his family, to know that regardless of your past, it is always possible to triumph with no need to inherit adversity. You choose your own destiny. Son Bobby lives nearby, daughters Tammy and Margaret further away in Oklahoma and California, *"each carried in my heart proudly."* FourSpeed and Donita took care of a lot of lost and lonely kids when they were younger. Any child who needed a home was welcome.

~

"The good, the bad and the ugly: I guess if we're honest we've all had our moments. In my youth I made mistakes but since then I feel as a father I am nothing short of excellent, if I can say so without sounding like a jerk. I don't get to see my daughter nearly as much as I'd like

but the distance is there, nothing I can do about that, and I work a lot and I do mean a lot. My kids know I'm here for them for anything, it's all good. And family isn't all about blood. Family is family, doesn't matter how it came about. There are not many I let within my walls but once they're inside, they are there for good."

One might assume at first glance, with a body full of tattoos, and his rough-around-the-edges look, that FourSpeed was a long-haired hippie from the 1960's, possibly strung out on drugs or dealing with alcohol addiction. However, once he begins to talk, that preconception is killed immediately. Quite the opposite is true, in fact, FourSpeed, a proud vegetarian, may be regarded by some as somewhat of a "health nut." When asked if drugs or alcohol are a problem in his life:

"I did my share of drugs and alcohol when I was young but walked away from that lifestyle. Best thing I ever did in some ways I guess. I see others around me still caught up in drink and drugs and it's really sad. As a young person, it's fun and games and party on, but later in life you're just an old drunk or druggie. Some just can't or won't grow up I guess. Their business and choices just don't make sense to me. I can still go hang in the bars and shoot pool or hang with buddies, doesn't bother me. Must admit I wonder how some of the fools get home afterwards."

When I read that statement, I thought "That is SO FourSpeed," because he always considers the end result of his actions, unlike many who get caught up in the phony highs that drugs supply. I remember reading quite a few conversations on the VBMO forum that would have escalated into violent discussions had it not been for FourSpeed interjecting his own insight and opinion. My guess is he is a good mentor to any young people who cross his path or spend any amount of time with him. He has wisdom to impart.

~

"I attended some college, studied books and stuff. I went to work when my wife got pregnant and haven't had the time to go back, or so I say. I'm an avid reader and that

has been my bedrock all my life. I find it strange when people don't read. Guess you could say I'm still studying. Pieces of paper on the walls, sorry, none here."

I have questioned FourSpeed about certain issues over the course of our online friendship and have never gotten a hasty answer. His replies to me are always serious, sensible, and thought-provoking. A student of life and a fan of the written word, FourSpeed needed no college degree to prove he has a brain. In fact, I consider him one of the most intelligent people I have ever met. One of the qualities most endearing to me is his ability to see through anyone's bullshit. I learned pretty quickly that nobody pulls anything over on FourSpeed. There are very few in his class.

~

"I've worked construction all my life, everything from shipyards in my youth to refineries and chemical plants as an adult. I'm a pipe welder by craft, worked union and non-union, it's all the same, and they both have their pros and cons. Last several years I've been on a computer, something I latched onto when someone I knew was going to 'drag up.' People knew my skills as a web designer so I was asked to step in. Can't complain, the AC is nice on those hot Texas days and I've always been into computers since the day my older brother turned me on to them back in the DOS days. I do wish I could take a real vacation; I've been working all my life and never really just taken off. It's always tomorrow, next year."

FourSpeed maintains a strong presence on the internet, as there are several friends, after many years, who continue to stay in touch with him. Meeting him through the VBMO was a lucky day for me. People who are well-read are usually very good at writing and expressing their thoughts, which I noticed about him right away. It was always a delight when I would receive an email from FourSpeed because it would never be something trivial or insignificant. Any discussions we have are intellectual and any criticism from him is constructive. I value his opinion and he knows this.

Even though he has been close to death *"a few times, we'll just leave it at that,"* FourSpeed has no fears in this life.

~

"Absolutely nothing scares me; I've never even found a movie (one of my favorite movies is 'Natural Born Killers') that could scare me. Fault maybe, I don't know. Criminals don't inspire me and all the sugar coating in the world won't change the bottom line."

His priorities are his family, good friends, and his freedom. He credits Donita, the love of his life, for standing by him through every misfortune and keeping him together when depression loomed ahead.

~

"I can fall in love on a whim but my one true love who's always been there no matter what is my lady, Donita. She's been a rock in my life. She's as much a part of me as taking a breath. I have several people that I hold near and dear that I'd do anything for. A best bud that I'd take a bullet for, and she knows it. Yeah, a SHE. This old biker has a female best bud. Never saw that one coming but it happened and it's been freaking super cool. I think we both sit back now and then and think, wow this is certainly different but it works for us, great friend she is. Maybe it was the different worlds that we come from that drove us together so tight. I think most people know once I'm a friend, I'm a friend for life and there are some I've never even eyeballed that know I'd have their back. I'm loyal to a fault and love life and the people I choose to be with. Yeah, I can fall in love on a whim but that means different things to different people. Take it or leave it."

I have been to Texas four times in the last 10 years and I attempted each of those times to arrange to meet FourSpeed in person. The problem was I was in the Dallas/Ft. Worth area and he was four-five hours south of that location, and because my time was limited, it just never worked out. The other major factor was that FourSpeed, as long as I've known him, has worked constantly. I can't recall him taking any vacation time, except to visit his son or daughters.

~

"I haven't finished my ink and I work too much. I've lived a good life. Wish I'd gotten more formal education. Just wasn't in the cards or the bank account. Excuses, perhaps, as many do it with less, but that's just the way it is for me."

It is no wonder then that FourSpeed's major means of transportation is his motorcycle. For many years, he rode an early 1978 Shovelhead, bought new in March 1978, one of the last with points before they went over to the electronic ignition. He calls his Shovel "BB." However, he retired BB in 2005 and she's currently being rebuilt from the frame up. Since then, FourSpeed bought a 2005 Night Train that he currently rides (he says maybe it's because of his age now that he's enjoying not having to wrench as much).

~

"I just about ride every day of my life and I do mean every day. It's as much a part of me as my arms but I don't get any great spiritual experience out of it. I just ride, as I've always done. I ride because I love riding and don't care much for cars and trucks and it's too damn far to walk. Unlike some brand snobs, I'd ride a Moped if that's all I had. I just ride."

FourSpeed's love of motorcycles is succeeded by his son and daughter, who both own their own bikes and learned from their father that it is wiser, when taking control of the handlebars, to also learn to take control of the care and maintenance of your machine. The road is no place for careless mistakes but accidents can and do happen. FourSpeed's philosophy is not to rely on others for help unless absolutely necessary. The rider who can take care of himself in an emergency is the one most confident and respected among his peers.

~

"There's book smart and street smart and everything in between. My views on wisdom might be my neighbor's joke. It's all in perspective."

FourSpeed is a fascinating man in many ways. One of the characteristics that sets him apart is his courage to hold onto his beliefs, no matter how contrary to the people around him who might otherwise influence his decisions. We would all like to believe that in times of trouble, we would stand our ground against an enemy, or that we would not hesitate to defend others, against popular opinion. FourSpeed has the will to persist in his beliefs. He may be challenged but faces his opponents with his strong convictions. I am grateful for his friendship and feel very privileged to have been able to share part of his life through our "virtual" worlds.

~

"Just ride, don't box yourself in with labels, brands or any of that nonsense. Treat those you meet with the respect you would want shown to you or your family. Sometimes it's that one kind word people remember years later in life. Don't know who said it but it fits: "I never learned anything while I was talking."

FOURSPEED

* JUST WHEN I THOUGHT I WAS OUT, THEY PULL ME BACK IN *

~

Old friends: when one disappears from your life and you hear nothing from him/her for years, it is easy to fall into that fog of forgetfulness. Have you heard from him? Not since whatzisname's funeral, blah, blah, blah. Then...BANG! A friend randomly reappears when you least expect that to happen, and the re-connection begins.

Those old feelings start creeping around, like distant footsteps in the hallway that get louder and louder with every hour spent together. Coffee a few times a week becomes a psych session where you are both sharing things you haven't even thought about in years. You spend time reminiscing, laughing, and crying at how naïve and foolish you once seemed and how carefree life was so long ago.

Sooner or later you confront the inevitable obstacles that friendship tosses in your path. Do you climb those mountains together or struggle to the top alone? If your friend's mountain is higher than yours, is this the time to abandon him at the bottom so that you can continue to pursue your own personal peak and go on your merry way? Some may be able to follow that trail, but quoting one wise philosopher: "Friendship is felt through the heart, not seen by the eyes," a true friend, as most *bikers* prove to be, absolutely cannot walk away from a wounded brother. The heart does not allow it and to be haunted by negligence would be a great cross to bear. This has been documented over and over by the countless brothers who have been wrongly (or rightly) convicted and still have the support from their family and friends in the biker community.

Borrowing a quote from "Godfather III": "Just when I thought I was out, they pull me back in," may describe the sentiment of re-discovering a part of your past. As can be experienced when an old friend comes back into your life and you start to "re-learn" that kind of love, some feelings never die even if you try to kill them. Time may halt but can never erase what has been imprinted on a soul.

* THANKS TO BIKERS FOR GIVING *

~

Take some time to reflect on all that bikers do and have done in years past, for their local community and even national organizations. The bikers of New York State, and all around the world, have gone above and beyond to help when they could, and there are always numerous events scheduled which benefit some charitable cause.

The Sons of Sam Motorcycle Club from Syracuse, New York, for example, was founded by veterans for the sole purpose of supporting members of the U.S. military, past, present, and future. Every event sponsored by the club benefits veterans in some way. While on the subject of the military, there are members of Rolling Thunder who organize the Patriot Flight biker escorts for WWII Veterans when they are finally able to visit the WWII Memorial in Washington, D.C. The Veterans Motorcycle Club sponsors a Homeless Veterans Run as well as a Christmas party every year for homeless vets in the Albany area.

The "We Care Ride" was held during recent years to benefit the Crohn's & Colitis Foundation, and has raised well over $20,000 to aid in research and to help local families struggling with the disease. The Boozefighters Motorcycle Club (Chapter 60) sponsors "Bikers Fight Hunger" every November, filling a local food pantry in Troy, New York, which is so desperately needed at that time of the year. Also, in Central New York, the local biker clubs in that area collected enough donations to feed 500 families on Thanksgiving.

It is not always about food pantries or charities, however. In September of 2010, after a huge fire which destroyed the Blackthorne Resort during the Catskill Mountain Thunder Motorcycle Festival, the bikers there pulled together and not only ensured that no one was hurt during the tragedy, but also donated money to help the exchange students who were employed at the Resort and had lost everything they owned that weekend. In October, proceeds from the *New York Rider*

Magazine Fifth Year Anniversary Bash were donated to Gilda's Club. And let's not forget a most unexpected show of support back in 2006 in another state, when over 3,000 bikers rallied in support of the Amish school shooting victims in Lancaster, Pennsylvania.

While this article highlights only a few events that have occurred in years past, there are countless occasions at which the motorcycling community plays a huge part in the successful outcome. While counting your blessings for your health, your family and friends, please include a thank you to the bikers in this world who support all of us, even as many of their contributions and their compassion remain unacknowledged or simply unknown.

~

HANK McGRATH
* Righteous *

"No one will ever truly be free unless they redefine their lives to mark and create their own personal strategy for successful liberty, and no one shall be called a hero who does not represent the age-old adage that we are here as adults to lay down firmer ground for the next generation."

Life is easy for some people. For others, the face in the mirror every morning reminds the bearer of a lifetime of terrors that remain intact. The nightmares should be over, yet they still threaten to steal into the empty, vulnerable spaces that continue to plague the victim. So it is for Hank McGrath, a man who has suffered unimaginable pain, yet is able to hide the scars from most of his acquaintances. To the few who really know Hank, the wounds are wide open.

Hank McGrath is Executive Director of B.A.D. (Bikers Against Discrimination), and the Freedom Action League, a rabid host of the Biker LowDown Radio show and Spirit of Bikers radio, writer for news sources such as *New York Rider Magazine* or White Trash News, and is noted for being the first to issue an award from the President of the United States to one-percenter clubs in recognition for ALL clubs volunteering to benefit the community in worthy causes, particularly the Hells Angels Nomads New

York and the 69ers Motorcycle Club North Country Crew. He resides somewhere in a New York "hidden bunker" where he cares for his daughter, AlannaWillow McGrath, while working on issues directly related to bias and discrimination against bikers.

~

"Wisdom is within the winds, the breeze, known only to those who are chemically, biologically, physically, and spiritually ripe for the moment of wisdom's breath. Some of us breathe it in young by some initiating experience and it guides us like a conscience. Others redeem its qualities through reflection of memories gathered all in the right spot of our brain and impulse. Still others must suffer to "see" or survive what they felt to make sense out of the words that flow in their minds. Somewhere amidst the foggy forest of wisdom there is reason by which it comes to you – for some it is simple and natural to be wise or gather and accumulate internal wisdom, to others wisdom is not even a desire or consideration - they sloth around waiting to die by accident or on purpose."

Hank came into my world when he contacted me to inform us that he intended to present the Hells Angels and the 69ers Motorcycle Clubs with a Presidential Volunteer Award and he wanted us to witness the ceremony. That day in July 2008 was an historical event and would not have happened if not for Hank's persistence.

Upon meeting Hank, one notices immediately that he is friendly, outspoken, and a talker! The man can converse for hours on any subject and is especially politically well-versed. Hank's intelligence attracted me and to find that he is also a prolific writer seemed to seal the bond between us.

~

"At age 13 or 14, I got a ride on a Triumph Bonneville. To a kid, that's unforgettable! You're scared shitless thinking you are gonna' eat the pavement at high rate of speed...defenseless! Riding stirs the spirit and soothes the weary soul; but, for me, there was no greater spiritual experience in my life than to literally take the opportunity to rob officials and judges in Albany during the early 1980's (I led an armed raid into their private

party and took their money). That kind of spiritual rush experience (which I have had the pleasure of feeling a number of times) can be both powerful and meaningful to one's character. Then again, I have never had the opportunity to ride cross country and LIVE the "biker lifestyle" enough to enjoy that treasured experience so many seasoned bikers have told long tales about."

Hank does not ride a motorcycle but is included in this book for various reasons, one of which is his close association with one-percenter clubs in our biker community (Hank had to sell his bike to pay for a legal case to win custody of his daughter) and the fact he has the uncanny ability to strategically fight for rights while inspiring empowerment in the biker culture. That association inspired him to found Bikers Against Discrimination. B.A.D.'s mission is to support and educate bikers on their Constitutional rights, in a valiant effort to preserve the American biker culture, to re-educate the general public about the American biker culture and to check and balance government agencies and authorities regarding their persistent campaigns to harass, unjustly profile and discriminate against members of the biker culture.

Hank has been working with the Highwaymen Motorcycle Club on a civil rights case involving two of their club members. Through his diligent work investigating the legal process in conjunction with Highwaymen MC President, Steve Maley, he has acquired approximately 300 law books from Warren Redlick, Attorney and former candidate for New York State Governor. The books were donated on behalf of B.A.D. and the unjust convictions in the Tyler and Peeps case and will be kept in the first ever American Biker Law Library in Ilion, New York. Hank and Steve's vision is to provide access to the law library for bikers who seek legal information. Bikers will be encouraged and welcomed to use these books free of charge and if possible B.A.D. will also provide contact information for local biker attorneys and other legal resources available. The American Biker Law Library, dedicated to Tyler Maley and Joseph DeMatteo, is a One-percenter Biker Law Library which is open to all bikers/supporters and will be located at Steve's Custom Jewelry, 66 Otsego Street, Ilion, New York, (315) 894-4389.

~

"A primary principle of B.A.D. {Bikers Against Discrimination} is that the older and genuine clubs, many of which are one-percenters in spirit, are an essential element of American history. They are the key keepers for the origination and nature of the motorcycle culture. That is anthropologically TRUE and factually undeniable! On that basis, if I were to join a club I would do so with the interest of preserving that culture...and elevating to one-percenter – not join a club and create the façade that I am in some way a more legitimate citizen deserving of more rights than the one-percenter key keepers of the American Biker Culture!"

Just as the children of the wealthy are afforded certain advantages by virtue of their being born into such a lifestyle, Hank believes that if bikers were to procreate for the purpose of leadership, there would be far less oppression among the biker culture. If you are born into royalty and know nothing else, you are more or less destined for the throne. Children of wealthy parents have the option to attend the best colleges and universities, and are more likely to become doctors, lawyers, judges, etc. If the children of bikers are bred with a commitment by their parents to school them with the best education they can afford while exposing them to the biker culture, our society would benefit. Imagine a child who grows up knowing only the biker culture and becomes a Congressman. There are millions of bikers – the possibilities would be endless. Hank calls this his "Breed'em Out" campaign and his daughter, AlannaWillow, represents the first "Breed'em Out" child in America. In the meantime, electing people like factory workers, truckers, and other blue-collar workers, even if only 30% of their life experience is similar to yours, would result in a huge difference. This may be the answer to recuperating the America that once was. Wisdom is in the disadvantages, not by providing advantages. Hank has unique hands-on training and has been an active civil rights advocate for over 30 years. When Hillary Clinton's Senate seat was vacant, he actually ran for the U.S. Senate seat and was told his proposal was considered. He did not expect to be seated – he merely wished to convey the "voice of the people" and compel government to realize much of society would rather have someone of their own ilk representing them.

Hank started contributing articles for *New York Rider Magazine* and eventually began a monthly column titled, "Roads to Justice." The notion of a politically-focused column initially met with some resistance. Even though I was not as interested in the topics he chose, I saw the value in Hank's words and knew readers would welcome the information. Besides, I wanted to tap into his mind, even if a bit diabolical at times, because the truth is that Hank is a fascinating man with an unusual insight to offer to those who will listen. I was not disappointed.

Among the projects Hank is currently involved with are the Freedom Action League, which he created as a vehicle for distributing the President's Volunteer Award; Voices of the People, a TV and radio program which Hank founded as another avenue used to inform and educate the public on civil rights issues. He also produced and directed the award-winning cable TV documentary series, "Spirit of Biker Brotherhood," which covered the biker subculture and lifestyle as it actually is. In addition, during the last four years, Hank has been a major player on the Bikerlowdown, a radio show promoting the spirit of biker brotherhood, via the online media affiliate, Blogtalk Radio. Hank has most recently saved the BikerLowDown as archives for listeners and started the new "Spirit of Bikers" Radio Show. He also is editor and reporter for Olde Country News online and writes a column on Philosophy of Civil Rights in the Albany Examiner. He also has the informative site, FreeOnePercenter. com, where much of B.A.D.'s work is found. He organized a campaign with *New York Rider*, Russ Brown, BikerLowDown, B.A.D. Administrative Director Chuck DeCost of Alphabiker.com, and a number of others to shut down the Port Jefferson, New York proposal to "bar motorcycles and unsightly motorcyclists" from their community and has campaigned against New York State Police for their media propaganda that Hells Angels and other biker clubs are "criminal enterprises." He goes on to show how the Governor, State Police and others affiliated instead can be viewed as a "criminal enterprise."

~

"I graduated from high school while in prison. I went to the Junior College of Albany (Sage), pioneering the first

prison college release program in the State and years later
attended Skidmore College in Saratoga Springs. Then, a
number of years later, with accumulated credits and life
experience from the prior colleges, I completed a two- year
program with Canterbury University in Hyde-Cheshire,
Manchester, England (as a foreign student working on
projects such as the Sinn Fein political party in Northern
Ireland). I have a Bachelors Degree in Business Science."

Hank and I have spent time together at biker events and
meeting for a meal here and there, and after awhile he began
to intimate a little about his past. He revealed that he was
incarcerated for 27 years and considers himself a "child of the
system." This revelation did not scare me away or deter our
friendship from developing further, in fact, it brought us closer.
Now he felt even freer to discuss his years in jail, his rebel-
rousing escapades, and his opinions on everything. There were
moments when I would feel compelled to blurt out, "Hank, you
are making me exhausted, please shut up!"

~

"As a child, I am someone who suffered and survived being
drowned, tortured, starved, enslaved, chained and left for
dead dozens of times. As an adult, I survived being hit-
by-a-car-contract, being shot and stabbed, enslaved and
imprisoned, hated and loved. A defining moment in life
may be simply enjoying a cherry cheesecake or the cool
curves of a woman or relating to someone's freedom or
touching a tree and feeling it tremble...or having a child...
and last but not least – dying."

Because he was constantly trying to escape his violent home,
the "system" sent him to juvenile incarceration at 10 years old,
citing he was incorrigible for "chronic history of running away".
Hank was the victim of a severely mentally ill mother and a
distant father. He said she was quite like the woman in the movie
"Misery." There were other siblings (six from the same father, one
from a different father) and all suffered different degrees of abuse
by their mother. Hank ran away often and as early as five or six
years old. By 12 he found a way to get farther away - Pittsburg,
Pennsylvania. He took the bus by himself, slept in cars, and stole

things with other kids for food and money, but was eventually found and brought back to the "juvenile system" in New York. Besides being in detention homes for running away from his abuse, he was also sent to the House of Good Shepherd and the Tryon School for Boys from age 11 through 15, but would again begin the pattern of escaping. Hank was finally sent to prison after being arrested for a crime of robbery 3rd which consisted of fighting with a fellow criminal over money owed to him. Though his partner in crime did not press charges, the State picked up the charges and sent Hank to prison after emancipating him (making him a legal adult at 18). Hank was bright as a youth and self-educated. He took his High School equivalency test and passed with unusually high grades (his last formal grade was fifth). Hank spent the better part of the 1960's, 1970's and 1980's in juvenile facilities and prison, including Elmira Correctional Facility, Comstock ("gladiator school"), Clinton CF, Eastern CF, Attica, Green Haven and Coxsackie and was known as a very volatile "troublemaker," "striker," and organizer against the system. In between stints of imprisonment, Hank was an amateur boxer and sparring partner for a number of boxers like Marvin Hagler in Boston, Massachusetts. In later years, he was the middleweight champ in Green Haven Correctional Facility, known as "Hammerin' Hank," a moniker that sticks with him on radio today. Besides his own experiences as a fighter, Hank is quick to mention how his uncle, Dave Zyglewicz of Watervliet, New York, was a promising heavyweight until he suffered an industrial accident in the 1960's. Ziggy fought Frazier in 1968 (who for many years owned "Ziggy's" in Watervliet and whose wife, Fran, owned a popular biker bar, Mother's Roadhouse. Fran passed away in December 2010). Hank did media promotions on Latham's Danny Ferris and Catskill's Mike Tyson, was a member of F.I.S.T. with Larry Holmes and Gerry Cooney, and also promoted his own local heavyweight boxer in Albany named Hannibal Hood. As well, today, Hank actively promotes the passage of Ultimate Fighting in New York State and also helps to promote the Albany Boxing Gym which trains local youth's at 96 Quail St., Albany, New York, with Professional Boxing Trainer and cut man, Jerrick Jones, and Professional Boxing/ Kickboxing Trainer, Andy Faragon. By far, he is no stranger to the spirit of fighting!

"Growing up so young in the system without family or support except the historical attachment to my uncle Ziggy and the fact I was Irish, I had little choice but to keep my chin down and fists up, paving a history of survival and honor to my family name against all oppositions. Winning becomes defined as surviving. That's why I respected and understood Mike Tyson so well."

Hank shared a few of the details of his abusive childhood with me, and knowing there is deep pain embedded in his heart and mind was no surprise to me. My eyes could see the wounds and this only added to the paradox of this man. His pain does not need to be dictated to me because our connection enabled me to feel it. It is not pity I feel for Hank, never have, rather, I feel deep respect and admiration for someone who has survived by his own innate sense of faith and hope. Many would have collapsed under the weight of his bad memories. Hank chose to live on and redeem his soul. *"I believe in God. Does God believe in me?"*

~

"I am a media pioneer with idealistic foolery. I am a semi-retired armed robber, womanizer, con man, thug, hood, and was even an amateur boxer. I say "semi-retired" because I am older now and still need those traits to be successful in today's economy! It's just a different style in approach."

Hank uses his humor as a shield to protect him from exposing a blemished soul. A man with a less than stellar history, Hank will attempt to cloak himself in whichever robe suits his purpose. The jobs he has held throughout his free life serve as evidence of this. Assimilating himself into any situation and befriending strangers unaware is one element of his personal nature. He has a talent for the art of persuasion.

While in prison, Hank led successful, historical protests for prisoner's rights. He was also a legal advocate for gang members, the disabled, children of abuse and missing and exploited children and in father's rights today, believing that the American welfare system and elements of government have sought to replace the man, the family structure and the cultures of families as a way to control society. He has even volunteered himself to begin a hunger strike – the longest in New York State history, for bail reform in the early 1980's.

~

"My favorite movies are 'Cinderella Man' or 'Princess Caraboo' or 'The Count of Monte Cristo.' GREAT STUDY MATERIAL and strategy tools for dealing with life and the deceitful powers that be."

Family life became more important to Hank in later years. In his own words regarding his family:

"Close," for many, has different meanings and ways. We are clan-like in nature but that also means we branch out in distance and lifestyle. Some of us require a monthly check in, some ya don't hear from, just about, AND THAT'S CLOSE FOR US! "Family" may also take on a different shape for many in that being distant from members of direct family, we develop quality friends who, themselves, represent our core beliefs and share in what we do or how we live, just as family would. Friends become family."

However unlucky in love, Hank was not averse to delve into a traditional marriage (three times), yet he does not believe he has ever really loved anyone as they have deserved to be loved.

~

"I do not believe that I have ever been "in love." Never had that surrendering feeling people speak about relating to being in love. I will say that during the times in life that I loved myself, became more of who I am, balanced, I would seem to attract some of love's magic from badass women. Seems also that I have been attracted to attractive, highly sensual yet inwardly disturbed women which would make for a relationship filled with as much negative drama as there were nice or loving moments. That clouds one's ability to really become immersed in LOVE."

Hank's most meaningful marriage was with Linda Lee Willey-McGrath, a righteous and extremely attractive woman who passed away in his arms at home in November 2001. ***"She suckered*** *me in her last hour – had me promise her, GIVE MY HONOR, that I would use my criminal traits and bullshitting talents to help others. Having very little but my culture/heritage and honor to live by my word was "golden." I AGREED and gave my word several times, all the while thinking (she's just sick now, she'll get better and I won't have to be honorable there). She died in my arms an hour later. I sipped her last breaths into my body with HONOR! Helping others has made my life miserable even though I am able to redirect my inner desire to "start trouble" into "for the good of the masses."*

Hank's most recent union with a woman, Kayla Drinwater, a "true friend and deep partner in life," produced a child, AlannaWillow McGrath, for which Hank is eternally grateful, having been denied the experience of fatherhood during his younger years. *"Years ago, I dated a woman who was separated from her husband, got her pregnant (which was a complete highlight for me) and during the same period her and her husband got tight again, she agreed to an abortion (I knew nothing about at the time). She also agreed with state authorities who were investigating me (for alleged criminal ties and activities) that I was now a danger to her...she helped them set me up to go to prison."* Responsibility was now an absolute necessity instead of a notion he dabbled in occasionally. Suddenly the future was not his own. His priorities shifted to this precious gift he was given, to care for, love and nurture. The child brought a light to Hank's eyes. Hope was restored and some of the darkness was extinguished. His purpose was now clearly defined.

~

"I am a revolutionary, a strong Celt by nature, a man who believes with great vision in giving the energy of your life to battles and fights which seem unbearable and impossible to win. It is from within that vision and from that energy that I approach my child. 'Tis easy to give her love that she creates with me and just as easy to share with her the reasons to fight what I have given my life for – sanity! Long after I am gone the fires of my spirit will be seen through her eyes. Her first present from me was a stick and a stone. Today, two years later, she collects both.

We are Celts, first and foremost. Not "White." Our cultural
and meaningful impressions last forever within the soul
of a child, as will I. We are all existing to lay down firmer
ground for the next generation. My daughter has her own
unique and driven soul and I will challenge that so she
can define her life with great liberty and freedom."

During the 1970's, Hank worked in support of Sinn Fein, a political arm of the IRA and for the freedom of Ireland, as did many Irish-Americans here in the United States. In later years, he was visited in prison a number of times by the FBI warning him to end his support. He was also a long-time member of the Irish Northern Aide Committee. While in Northern Ireland, Hank organized and participated in a major peace march in Newry and Armagh. During that particular march he was unaware the knapsack he was wearing had a hole in it and a number of new Irish Republican Army support T-shirts began to fall out onto the ground behind him. The front of the T-shirt's was imprinted with IRA snipers or sayings like the following: *They may kill the Revolutionary but never the Revolution.* Anglo-Irish soldiers with machine guns seized Hank immediately out of the parade, led Hank into an apartment building hallway, and proceeded to search him for weapons as well as grill him for information. Eventually, Hank was released as they took him away in a military vehicle and ordered him to leave the country as soon as possible.

Hank became involved with support of Sinn Fein and the Irish Freedom Movement at an early age because he is Irish, from a strong Irish background and an Irish neighborhood in South Troy, New York. Throughout his youth he did not have any greater form of personal identification than his culture and heritage. When he became an unjust subject of the system he longed to be part of the IRA and return to the country of his grandfather and great grandfather. Unbeknownst to many readers, especially from the Capital District of New York, Hank is seen most every year marching amongst the Grand Marshall and Ancient Order of Hibernians holding the flags of Ireland's counties with great honor and has been a Marshall in the parades in New York City. To this day, Hank stated with conviction that if he were called, he would leave this country in support for the freedom of Ireland, as most Irish promised to do prior to leaving their mother country to America. Ireland's last King, Brian Boru, would knight everyone as Irish, regardless of race, culture or background, before a battle. Hank follows the same tradition with B.A.D. Every biker and club member who fights for the preservation and protection of the biker culture is an Honorary Member of B.A.D.

Hank's criminal background and life in prison for so many years forced him to learn how to defend himself. Indeed, he managed to survive a series of misfortunes that almost led to his destruction.

~

"I fell out in a coma days after an amateur fight, had a punctured lung (stabbed with an ice pick) and bled internally, chopped with a machete stuck in my head, starved to the point of pains, beaten for dead and thrown in a trunk once and some Columbians attempted to whack me (got a lot of 'em). Experienced facets of death, being turned inside out in seconds from somewhere deep inside the energy of your soul, the pains so searing that it becomes flashes of light OVER feeling, the complete turn off of the brain, just hollow sounds with no thoughts, but you survive."

Despite his abnormal and unfortunate upbringing, Hank makes no attempt to hide his faults, in fact he boasts about the weaker aspects of his disposition which inevitably molded him into the man he became. He is quick to admit his failures, his weaknesses and his disconcerting temperament, but stands firm regarding the evolution of his character.

It is very hard to understand why or how, but somewhere in his soul, when his mother died, Hank found the grace to forgive her. He wrote a beautiful Eulogy which he delivered at her funeral.

~

"I am great – with all my faults, misfortunes and misjudgments. They are like jewels compelling me to at least attempt to define life. I am small because of the fact I am caught in dimensions of time, either it's the right moment or the wrong moment, either I know what I am doing or I did not create the circumstances I now suffer,

helpless and capable only of dreaming of being ready for the right moment and PRESTO, I won the lottery or an armored car vehicle starts spilling thousands all over the highway, or I am with the same woman for 10 years and she really enjoys and loves to share oral sex. That's the raw extent of my character! I expect the same raw reality out of others. The more unique and real, the more righteous."

In response to the question of whether he suffered problems from substance abuse: *"In this odd character I have developed through life's impulses, I never suffered drug or alcohol addictions even though there is very little I have NOT used or experimented with. A factor in this may be that I "used" at a much earlier age than most and we may also consider the probability that the drugs used may have actually enhanced my pain threshold, intuitiveness and persistence to survive what thousands of others have not. I also lived (from childhood on) each day of my life (and today) keenly aware that a "system" would always pursue me on top of the personal knowledge that police, judges, prosecutors, and government officials heavily used either drugs or alcohol or both. The contradictions evident to me about life actually influenced my "choices" to not be like them...a contradiction."*

My impression of Hank is that he is a strong man with a wealth of idle talent. He is extremely intelligent and perceptive. While you realize his potential you also regret you discovered it. It is possible once in awhile, to probe deep enough to uncover the restless spirit he holds within his heart. His freedom now is spent helping others achieve the same liberty. Hank welcomes strong debates and will often be the first to volunteer his expertise to anyone in need of an advocate. The work he has already done for bikers, namely coordinating the first B.A.D. Support Jam in 2009 with his brother, Chuck DeCost of AlphaBiker.com, at the 69'ers MC NCC clubhouse in Troy, New York, which was very well attended by club members and non-club members, has opened doors for bikers who had previously been unaware of their own rights and the simple fact that motorcycle clubs are legal entities. Also in 2009, Hank led a campaign to inspire bikers across the country to support the concept of "culture" (American Biker Culture) and request it be included in the protection clause of each state's Human Rights Laws. He submitted the same proposal to New York State and forges ahead. The unique idea is that if "culture" is included in the Human Rights Laws those in the American Biker Culture would have better legal grounds to fight for equal rights. Now in his 50's, Hank still has much to accomplish and works tirelessly toward the many goals on his horizon. His self-imposed tasks are daunting but he accepts the challenges with vigor.

At the time of this writing and as an example of Hank's unique angst and ability to act powerfully and strategically, he has submitted a State Habeas Corpus seeking injunctive relief from the Patriot Act and the National Defense Authorization Act of 2012 (NDAA) that was passed on December 31, 2011. This act allows for internment of United States citizens who are "belligerent to the government", which Hank believes directly targets citizens and groups like those in the American Biker Culture. He submitted an addendum with the Habe which argues how bikers are not equally protected by civil/human and Constitutional rights in America (and New York State) and therefore are unjustly subject to further violations to their citizenship by the passage of this act against U.S. citizens.

~

"My only regret will be if I die before the revolution - when rights are equally applied to all. When an Irishman dies there's no more bullshit, no more lies, no more bills, no more government, no more fighting. It's kind of a thing to celebrate (Irish Wake). Especially when tax collectors and government agents show up to make sure you're dead, like at my father's funeral. It's honorable! I don't want to be reborn as a politician or lawyer or official. How shameful that would be. Hopefully, I will come back as a wolf or coyote 'cause then the game's still on and the fight is still there...to survive.
That is the spark of life – to survive!"

After learning about Hank's life and all he has been through, I asked him what keeps him going and from where he draws his strength. His answer, following a long pause, was, *"I still believe in magic."*

~

"To be responsible for the future and be free at the same time requires both the desire and willingness to defeat the enemy/challenging life circumstance while defending the liberties of others. Define your purpose with every choice. We are all here, as adults, to lay down firmer ground for the next generation...In the AMERICAN BIKER CULTURE!"

HANK McGRATH

(with AlannaWillow McGrath)

* I WAS NOT BORN ON A BIKE *

~

I was not born on a bike. If you've been around bikers long
enough, you've no doubt heard someone, somewhere, say, "he's
not a *real* biker." What, you don't ride a Harley? You're not a
real biker. You don't own a Shovelhead? You're not a real biker.
You don't ride in the rain? You're not a real biker. You don't live
"the lifestyle"? You're not a real biker. Blah, blah, blah! I am
not going to debate the real biker vs. non-real biker (whatever
that is). I am only going to speak my peace.

I saw a fantastic cover band for "Queen." The singer who
impersonates Freddie Mercury is Gary Mullen and listening to
him was like hearing Freddie Mercury sing from the grave. It
was eerie and really cool at the same time. I always regretted
not seeing Queen in concert when they were in their heyday, so
it was fun for me to go back in time and relive my teenage years,
even if only for two hours. There were diehard Queen fans in
the audience (I could tell by the way they reacted when the show
began), and I'm sure a lot of them got pretty emotional by the end
of the show. Then there were fans like me – not a diehard Queen
fan, but a fan who always admired Freddie Mercury's amazing,
almost operatic voice, and his flamboyant stage persona. That
must be extremely difficult to replicate, yet Gary Mullen does it,
seemingly naturally, and with a deep respect for the deceased
Freddie. In the end, though many may criticize this band for
trying to resurrect an icon, they are making a lot of people
happy. Isn't that the point?

My husband and I did not start riding motorcycles until after
we were married, had kids and were pretty much settled. Most of
us get to a point in our lives when we have a little extra time and
newfound energy (from not having to change diapers and haul
baby carriers around anymore), and seek opportunities to simply
have fun. Riding a motorcycle was our answer to that quest.
Dino and I always had a fondness for motorcycles and dreamed
of one day being able to spend time riding, so this was really
just the fulfillment of that lingering, unspoken dream. We've
met many people since starting to ride – from bike mechanics

and motorcycle magazine editors, publishers, bike builders, the American Chopper Show cast and crew, Hells Angels and other club members, to everyday people like us just enjoying the ride. Through the years, I've heard, read, and participated in a few debates about the perception of a real biker. This subject always generates a lot of anger which I can understand, but it's also unbelievably ridiculous how much energy people put into it. Who really cares what you ride, how you ride, or who you ride with, unless it affects you personally?

There are some bikers who just don't like to see others enjoying themselves on a bike, especially if those others took a 'shortcut' by not having ridden a bike since they were old enough to tie their shoes. (You can't be as happy as me, I've been riding a Harley since I was ten. You're not a real biker, you are just a motorcycle *enthusiast,* and don't you forget it). Fine. Big deal. Call me whatever you like. I'll still be riding behind, in front of, or alongside you whether you like it or not, because I like to ride. Isn't it funny that some bikers segregate themselves this way? It's funny but it's not funny because it really is defeating the whole idea of brotherhood and camaraderie that bikers are notorious for, or claim to be. I know all bikers don't think this way, but there are enough of them around to have an impact. We are all on this earth for however many years we are lucky to live; some of us ride cars, some of us ride motorcycles, and some of us ride both (by the way, if your main source of transportation is a 'cage', then you're not a real biker). All bikers need each other – there is power in numbers. We need those numbers to keep multiplying, to continue advocating for bikers' rights and for increasing the mere presence of motorcycles on the roads. The more the merrier, the more the safer, the more the stronger.

Whether you were born on a bike or just started riding last week, we have two commonalities: 1. We love to ride. 2. Riding makes us HAPPY. I think we would be wise to remember that the club members you might encounter around the corner from the 'posers' who irritate you to no end, and the group of weekend warriors down the road, are all riding because it makes them *happy*, not because they are trying to impersonate a 'real' biker.

I know Gary Mullen is not Freddie Mercury. I know Elvis is not alive and well out in Vegas, and I think most people can tell the difference between someone who is new to riding and someone who is a seasoned professional. Why waste time trying to divide ourselves, just enjoy the ride and meet as many other bikers as possible, jaded or not.

We don't all fit into one category, and that's ok, in fact, it's good. Call me a poser and I'll call you an ass for taking yourself too seriously. It doesn't matter if we were born into the lifestyle, if we bought the bike yesterday or we've been riding since we were ten years old. We all belong to the real 'club' called "riders." Don't worry, be happy, and get out and ride!

~

* **BIKER CHICKS** *

~

For the past five years or so, I have been the Editor of *New York Rider Magazine*, and have met hundreds of bikers, primarily from the Albany area to Syracuse, Newburgh, and New York City. My endearment to bikers is no secret to my friends or my readers. However, I don't think I ever addressed the topic of my *female* biker friends (I use the term "biker chicks" with great affection).   Who says "biker chicks" are rough, tough bitches who could care less about anyone but their 'old man'? I have to admit that when I was a kid and used to see bikers and their women parked outside of Dunkin' Donuts, they intimidated me a little, and I couldn't help thinking, "wow, I wouldn't want to mess with them...," but that all goes back to the perception people have when they see a bunch of boots and black leather jackets. Then again, having been a victim of "weight discrimination" myself over the years, I learned quickly never to judge by a cover. There were many who might have been my friend had they been able (or willing) to see under my surface. The wise ones did, and they are my lifelong friends. Kindred souls seem to find each other in this world sooner or later.

It is within the biker culture that I have seldom, if *ever*, encountered the type of judgmental people that I knew in the past. This is especially true of the women, the "biker chicks" who ride their own bike, or are girlfriends, wives, or friends of bikers. In my opinion, these women are the most non-judgmental females on the planet. The many I have met and the few who have grown close to me have been the most loyal friends to me and I feel lucky to know each of them. They honestly could care less if I am short, tall, fat, skinny, or how much money I make. Everyone is regarded as a "brand new book" to a biker, waiting to be read and understood. We all know that good books are unforgettable and always recommended.

When I learned that my father was diagnosed with a serious disease, it was a very emotional time for me and my biker friends were among the first to offer me words of encouragement and comfort. These are the "real moments" of my life that make me so very proud to be part of the biker world. My hope is that those who still classify bikers as rough, tough, uncaring people, will open their eyes and discover the unexpected truth.

~

JB
* Faith *

"The most defining moment in my life came when I was 34 yrs. old. Drugs and alcohol had gotten the better of me. I had walked out on a wife and two children. I ended up in a rooming house alone and with a gun."

JB is a member of the Melchizedeks Motorcycle Club. I have seen JB at many of the biker events I attend and have gotten to know him and his wife, Cher, over the past few years.

I first heard of the Melchizedeks when they proposed a monthly "Biker Prayer" submission to *New York Rider Magazine*. Carmella and I both thought it was an excellent idea. During the summer of 2010, the Melchizedeks invited me to a "biker weekend" which was held at Grace Fellowship Church in Latham, New York, at which the founder of the Melchizedeks, Mark Ammerman, would be telling his story and relating the history of the club. I attended the ceremony and listened carefully to the presentation. The Melchizedeks are a Christian motorcycle club dedicated to spiritually serving the motorcycle community. Melchizedek is known as a King in the Bible and the color chosen for their patch, green, signifies life. Pastor Ammerman closed his sermon by quoting a passage from Genesis 50:20: "You intended to harm me, but God intended it for good to accomplish what is now being done, the saving of many lives." Melchizedeks MC members attend biker events and minister to those who express a need or desire to learn about Jesus Christ. They don't pressure and don't preach, but they make their presence known. Several of my friends have shared their experiences with the Melchizedeks and bear witness to the influence they have had in saving their lives. I know that this is only possible if the counselor fully understands the struggle. Many Melchizedeks members have hit rock bottom themselves and with the help of God, have turned their lives around.

When JB realized he had nowhere else to turn, and didn't have what it took to pull the trigger, he finally surrendered his heart and mind to the Lord and was blessed with the gift of forgiveness and hope for the future. JB credits his new life to his deep faith in God's promise and his relationship with his fellow disciples. He has never regretted his decision and his love of God and his family sustains him.

~

"I was 13 years old the first time I rode a motorcycle. Bikes and the biker culture have always been a part of me. When I'm riding on a winding road and smelling all the smells of nature, and in awe of the beauty that surrounds me, I can't help but know that God is riding with me and all this is His creation. I've never felt closer to Him then at these moments."

JB felt the Lord was pulling him toward a ministry and he was driven to share his revelation of Christ's love with the biker culture. What better way to fulfill that calling than to join a bike club of like-minded people who have been called for the same purpose. He decided to join the Melchizedeks MC, a group of men whose mission was the same. Each brings his own gifts to the table and they work together to use their abilities to counsel or console their "broken" brothers and sisters in the motorcycle community, as well as to nourish those who already accept the love of Christ. Having taken a few Bible courses in college only enhanced his gift for this vocation. JB considers it a blessing to be able to serve out of love, to a culture he loves. JB also works as a toolmaker at General Electric Research & Development Center.

~

"I measure my character by the choices I make and how I live my life daily. I try not to judge anyone and I surround myself with people of a like mind."

My personal experience with the Melchizedeks "in action" has been at the annual Catskill Mountain Thunder Motorcycle Festival in Durham, New York, every Fall. Together with members of the Christian Motorcycle Association, they arrive equipped with everything necessary to serve, physically and spiritually, the bikers and vendors who come to spend the weekend at the Blackthorne Resort. These people are in no way overbearing but they do let it be known that they are there for us if we need them. Instead, they extend a subtle invitation to break bread with them at every meal, and provide a respite from the routine and sometimes chaotic atmosphere of the rally. This is how the Melchizedeks minister –sharing the gentle but mighty power of Christ with His followers, yet quietly persevering through their mere presence in the biker community.

~

"What scares me is the thought of people leaving this world without having Jesus in their hearts"

It is wonderful to step away from the flurry of activities and enjoy some coffee and quiet conversation with the Melchizedeks. They don't forget you once you leave their camp. JB and Cher will reach out to you and invite you back, by the way, with no expectation of reward or payment. They share their food and drink freely and there is no discrimination as to who may join the feast. There are some people who seem to glow, possess an inner peace, and that peace emanates from them when they are near. I feel that peace when I'm around JB and his wife.

~

"I am an Advisor to my children."

JB describes himself as an advisor to his children (two daughters and one son). He may at one time never have given himself that label and although he regrets the mistakes he's made and abandoning his family, he knows that the grace of forgiveness has taught him to be a better man and teacher to his children and grandchildren. My guess he is one of those "fun" grandpas, with nine grandchildren to spoil.

~

"You can't get age and experience without suffering and surviving, together they equal wisdom."

"I guess as any man would say, I have a lot of regrets. But I choose to use mine as life experiences and without those regrets I wouldn't be where I am today." JB learned all he needed to know when he dug deep down into his soul and found the strength to change his life and walk with God. There is no wisdom so pure and priceless.

~

"Every Saint has a past and every Sinner has a future!"

JB

* BIKERS AND RELIGION *

~

Bikers are religious even if they're not religious. Some will say they have "found religion" somewhere along the line, others will say they were brought up in whatever faith they practice, still others will state that they don't believe in God at all.

One major characteristic of bikers is that they believe in the word "brotherhood." They call each other brothers, they treat each other like brothers, and that concept is the one most respected.

Many people, when faced with a crisis in their life, turn to religion for strength. There you find hope and faith, the things so necessary when all other resources have been exhausted. However, religions also hold "brotherhood" as one of their greatest commandments. Most motorcycle clubs have meetings periodically which they call "church" because they are mandatory meetings, and are usually, but not always, held on Sundays. These meetings are not only meant to address club business, but also serve as a fount of unity and renewal. Without gathering together occasionally, the club (or brotherhood) would eventually begin to unravel as their union is severed and each member becomes more distant from each other.

The parallels between religion and bikers are interesting when considering the essence of their convictions. Most religious denominations believe in unity and stress the importance of worshiping together. Bikers are proud to belong to a culture that connects people of all ages simply for the love of riding and the camaraderie inherent to that culture. The crux of most religions is to love and respect each other. This love encompasses love of family, friends, neighbors, and yes, "brothers." No doubt many bikers, though they may declare themselves atheists, do indeed practice the fundamental ideals of religion without even knowing it.

No one should be criticized for their principles. Whatever gets you through the rollercoaster of life is infallible, and despite what anyone tells you, what *you* believe is *your* true religion.

~

* BIBLE BIKER CLUB *

~

While studying the four gospels in a theology class, some interesting thoughts came to mind. As usual, my mind began to wander and I tried to imagine each of the gospel characters as bikers. Without getting into too much religious detail, the distinct personalities of each author is revealed as their stories are read. Perspectives are very different in each case (please accept my Catholic perception).

Let's imagine Jesus Christ (JC), Mark, Matthew, Luke and John as members of the Gospels Motorcycle Club, with JC of course as Club President. John would be Vice President since he was considered the right-hand man and provides a unique perspective, focused on divine ideals and ambitions (everything a President needs in a Vice-President). Matthew would be Sgt. at Arms since he frequently addresses issues of authority and discipline, and many regard Matt's as the "teaching gospel." Without question, Luke would be the Secretary/Treasurer, since he was inclined to recording all the details with as much accuracy as possible. Finally, Mark would serve as Road Captain. Although Mark does talk about Jesus' journey, he prefers to get right to the point, concentrating on the final destination (JC's Passion).

Reflecting on the characters I am familiar with in Albany motorcycle clubs, there are some parallels to the players in the Bible, at least as far as personalities and strengths are presented, and the fact that they are grouped together because of a common love. Would it be so far-fetched to believe that these men, if living today, might very well be bikers in their own special club? As followers of Jesus Christ, they "go against the grain," choosing to ally themselves with this radical stranger among them. They all took risks, as bikers do, but chose to believe that the journey they take will be worth the conflict (or persecution). They work together for the good of their club and its message (Veterans MC's, Christian MC's, and many others), participating in charitable acts, as bikers have always done.

~

MARDO
* Confidence *

"Riding a motorcycle for the first time almost scared me because I WASN'T scared!"

Mardo may not remember this, but the first time we actually met was when Dino was doing a photo shoot for a *New York Rider Magazine* calendar. We were at Ashe's Hotel in Warrensburg, New York, and Mardo was there to be part of another photo which included a few members of local clubs. To this day, I don't know why but I felt that someday he and I would become good friends. I never told him this; I just waited to see if it would really happen. Soon after that, Carmella asked me to do a story on the Highwaymen Motorcycle Club, so I seized my first opportunity to attend one of their events. I learned all about the history of the Highwaymen MC and spent a little more time talking to Mardo. After meeting the other members of the club, I decided from that day forward I would try to be at every Highwaymen MC event.

As time went on, I would find myself looking for Mardo at the biker parties because I was really starting to enjoy sharing a few beers and busting on him about his Irish-ness while he did the same with me about my Italian heritage. It wasn't long before I met his lady, Robin, and saw immediately why he loves her so much. Robin is a warm-hearted, beautiful person and I thank

Mardo for introducing us. She is a good friend who truly cares about the people in her life.

~

"Two major events changed my life: my motorcycle accident back in 1996 and the death of my nephew, Tommy."

Mardo was eight years old when he was introduced to motorcycles through two of his lifelong friends, Bubbles and Hotso. Bubbles owned a 5-horse Harley-Davidson mini bike and they used to go to Pigtown (South Troy) to ride. The next bike he rode was as a passenger on Jimmy Freehart's 550 Honda. Mardo knew then that he would own a motorcycle as soon as he could make it possible.

On April 20, 1996, Mardo was involved in a motorcycle accident, hitting a car head-on at 70 mph. He was thrown 25 feet in the air for 75 feet. He suffered dozens of fractures, endured 15 surgeries (five within the first 24 hours), died and was revived twice. He says he simply "drove outside of his capabilities." Still, Mardo got back on his motorcycle within three months of the crash, bungee-ing his crutches onto the back of the bike!

~

"I had to learn to live with pain on a daily basis."

Mardo came so close to death that I wonder how he survived and recovered with a wicked sense of humor while still in the hospital. He spent 32 days in Albany Medical Center following his crash until he was thrown out of the hospital and ordered to leave because he refused to follow doctor's orders. Besides ignoring the directives from the doctors and nurses, he refused to stop smoking pot outside in the "smoking hut" on hospital grounds. Mardo insists that his pain increased when he was forced to stop smoking pot. It also helped his mood and his appetite and he strongly believes marijuana should be legalized, at least for medicinal purposes. The head nurse from his floor caught him and made his life miserable, first having him confined to the floor, then to his room, until finally hospital administrators ordered him to leave. His friend, Tombo, rescued him from the hospital.

~
*"My only fear is of sharks and snakes -
I will not swim in the ocean."*

Mardo was devastated by the loss of his nephew, Tommy, who died at just 40 years old from colon cancer. Mardo has one brother and two sisters but he and his siblings are not close in age. As a result, he and Tommy developed a very close relationship. Tommy idolized Mardo, and they spent alot of time growing up together. After Tommy died, Mardo was drained of all emotion. His grief was a heavy burden and he numbed the pain (with drugs and alcohol) for months following Tommy's death. It was at this time in his life that Mardo earned his colors from the club. Mardo credits the club with saving him from self-destruction.

We never really "get over" the death of a loved one, and Mardo still gets choked up when he remembers Tommy. Mardo also recently lost his father. This time I was around to witness his grief and his heartbreak was transparent. The Grateful Dead's song, "Brokedown Palace," was his and Tommy's song and when he got the opportunity, he met Sunshine, Jerry Garcia's daughter, who graciously sang the song to him.

~
"Even though I know I could have done some things differently, I have always been very close to my kids and family is very important to me."

Mardo enlisted in the Army at 18, was out at 20, and landed his first job at Norstar Data Services. He eventually saved enough money to buy his first Harley-Davidson, a 1984 Sportster. Mardo was working at TransWorld Music when he met his wife and married in July 1990 and within a few years had two children, Liam and Meghan. He and his family lived in South Carolina for a short time until the company moved him back to New York to manage the local Record Town, and later, Strawberries. He stayed with the company until 1993 when once again he was fired for not conforming to the dress code policy. Mardo graduated in 1979 and attended several college classes in computer programming. He has had various jobs since leaving TransWorld. Mardo has one older brother and two older sisters.

His mom is still alive and he sees her whenever possible. Mardo cherishes his children and he has always been there for them when they needed him.

Mardo met Robin 25 years ago in 1987, through mutual friends. Robin was separated at the time. They had a steamy love affair for awhile but decided to go their separate ways. Robin remarried, divorced for the second time, and ran into Mardo again five years ago at an Eddie Money concert. Just a week following that night, they crossed paths again and talked for hours. They were fated to be together. I think this explains why "Quiet Man" is Mardo's favorite movie of all time (a man returns to his hometown to escape a past and finds love). Robin also helped Mardo work through the grieving process since they reunited just after Tommy's death.

~

"My 'Mardoism': If I don't like the taste, I can't swallow."

Mardo is loyal to a fault, but if something doesn't sound or seem right to him, he knows he cannot agree. Mardo admits that he may have a few enemies but that's alright with him. He figures that if someone is worth his time, they will eventually find a way into his world. He says that the people who crack the shell are his real friends. He surrounds himself with people who think and feel the same. He uses the analogy of a sand and rock sifter. The sand falls into the sifter but the rocky sand stays on top and stays together. We all have a common purpose and we (bikers) are all together for a reason. I knew that under Mardo's tough exterior there was much more to the man than meets the eye. Actually, I am honored that I was able to crack the shell and find the heart of this devil. That Mardo doesn't always "play well with others" and doesn't share his life freely just makes him even more intriguing. One of my proudest moments was when Mardo presented me with a plaque from the Highwaymen MC showing their appreciation for my support of the club through my writing.

~

"I would love to go to Ireland someday."

Mardo's grandfather is from Mooncain County Kilkenny in Ireland, although both of his parents were born in the United

States. Mardo has never been to Ireland himself and would love to visit someday. Another dream is to ride his bike out to Sturgis, South Dakota.

~

"For the first time in my life I felt like I belonged."

A friend brought Mardo to the Road Iron clubhouse, a local motorcycle club. Within an hour he could not believe that he was finally in a room with people who were just like him. Mardo decided to join the club and now can't imagine *not* being in a club. The Road Iron Motorcycle Club was shut down in 2006. After enjoying the freedom of no club commitment for a few months, Mardo attended a Hells Angels event and realized how much he missed that life. The best fit for him was the Highwaymen Motorcycle Club. He already knew some of the members through his association with the Road Iron MC. Mardo earned his Highwaymen MC patch in August of 2008.

~

"I was basically a messed-up individual until I joined a club."

Mardo's determination to join a motorcycle club was, according to him, one of the best decisions he's ever made. He believes it is a certain fate that brings biker brothers and sisters together. In Mardo's case, I believe joining a club was the only solution for him in order to find a "home" among the biker community. He is extremely proud to be a member of the Highwaymen Motorcycle Club and considers his membership a lifelong commitment. Mardo is an active participant in biker events and always conscious of his responsibilities with the club. His loyalty to the patch-holders of other local clubs does not go unnoticed and is respected by all.

~

"You can only have wisdom through age and experience."

Trust is important to Mardo and the trust from his friends and family combined with loyalty are the qualities he values above all. He admires a man who can demonstrate those character traits and convictions. Mardo was raised Catholic and went through the "whole shebang" – he was an altar boy, made his Communion, Confirmation, and raised his children the same way. As Mardo says, "A little church can't harm nobody."

~

"I love the personal isolation I feel on the bike. Riding is your own island, your own place, your own freedom, with your thoughts, things nobody can touch, that is you."

The gloves Mardo chose for this book are actually the right and left of two different pairs. He lost the right of one and the left of the other and decided to use them since both were favorites. He wears some impressive biker rings: three from the club, one made from the rings of women he has known, crafted into the Irish Claddagh. Mardo has about 20 tattoos over his body and all have meaning and significance.

Mardo is a man who exudes confidence and has proven to be a loyal friend to me. I am honored to be a part of his world.

~

"Just when life looks like easy street, there is danger at your door"....Jerry Garcia

MARDO

* BIKERS CAN'T BE STUFFED *

~

Having attended a wonderful gala one year, a benefit for a major charity foundation, a few things came to my mind while observing the participants. First, it's always nice to dress up but I am never totally comfortable in dress clothes. I really need my jeans, a sweatshirt or a hoodie to be "in my element." Still, I donned my only 'dressy' dress and joined my husband and friends for a night to remember. Strolling amidst ball gowns and thousand-dollar suits while sampling the "horse durvs," as my friend calls them, it was obvious to me that everyone was dressed to impress. Attendees were bidding on some very expensive items offered in the silent auction while I was mentally calculating the amounts in my mind and wishing for that kind of disposable income. How liberating that must be. Then again, maybe not. While eating our dinner, squished together at our beautiful table for ten, my friends and I were chatting and having a good time laughing with each other. We knew there was a speaker at the podium, and we were fairly low-key, however, apparently not low-key enough. Suddenly we all heard this big "SHUSH!!" from the table next to us. Glancing over, we saw five disapproving faces staring at us, silently admonishing us for being a bit too loud during our moment of merriment. I don't know about the others at my table but I felt like a very bad girl and expected to be sent out of the room any minute for misbehaving. Of course that did not happen, the "warning" was really very subtle, and everyone continued to enjoy the festivities. However, that is when a thought suddenly hit me – that this is why most bikers reject any strict conformity. Feeling as if you have to stifle yourself to the nth degree while enjoying a laugh with your friends really does rob you of a freedom, and that is not good. Oh, the rest of the night was wonderful, as we all realize the most important part of a night like that is sharing time with each other.

Now this is not to say that bikers are not a *refined* species, indeed they are, but you will have a hard time finding a "stuffy" biker! A friend told me recently that he felt funny sometimes in Barnes & Noble and when I asked why, he replied, "Well, because I'm more of a used-bookstore type of person." I laughed but my sentiments were similar on that night of the gala. I am more of a biker-bar type of person. Put me in a loud, rowdy biker bar and I know I'll have more fun than the stuffed suits and ball gowns. Variety is truly the spice of life though, and, as Cicero, the wise Roman author of ancient times, declared, "To Each His Own!"

~

* IT TAKES A BIKER *

~

My friend, Carmella Brown, and I were discussing one day the reasons she started *New York Rider Magazine*. Carmella has always said that the main reason she created *New York Rider Magazine* is because she felt that "bikers are the best people in the world and nobody knows it." So there we were talking about her philosophy and, by the way, I happen to agree with Carmella, which is why we get along so well. In no way are we saying that *all* bikers are nice, friendly creatures. As in any culture, there will be "bad pennies," but there are a lot of good deeds and worthwhile contributions that bikers make without anyone ever knowing (or noticing).

Take, for example, the "We Care Ride" that my husband and a few of his friends organized in years past, which I had personal experience with. That was no small feat and took a great deal of planning and a lot of footwork from all involved. The result was over 500 bikers participating and over $20,000 raised for the Crohn's/Colitis Foundation! This would never have been as successful if not for the generosity of bikers. "HOGS for Hospice" is another annual event that was pioneered by bikers. Every August the bikers in Albany, New York, sponsored by a local Harley Owner's Group and the local Hospice organization, round up for a day dedicated to the Hospice Foundation. Participants have gone above and beyond to help during that event and when questioned about why they give so much of themselves, they all shrug and say "It's for Hospice."

Many times during the riding season and even during the winter, you will find bikers sponsoring some charity event, either for a child who needs help or perhaps the family of a fallen brother. Don Birch, owner of the Sawmill Tavern in Schenectady, New York, fed the hungry and homeless every Sunday and the food was often donated by bikers from leftovers they had from a biker event that day or the day before! I cannot count the times I have heard of a biker crashing his bike and finding his biker friends immediately at his side or at the hospital, even before he's released from the Emergency Room. The same goes for the numbers that show up for a biker funeral. Support and brotherhood are never more apparent than at those times.

There was a man in Long Island who looked like a big, bad, mean biker, and before his sudden death, we learned that he was Santa Claus every year on Christmas Eve, visited every hospital he could get to in Long Island and delivered toys to sick children, at his *own* expense. When we were discussing this man, who insisted that his true identity never be discovered, I made the remark to Carmella, "Who *does* that kind of thing? Besides the rare selfless (or saintly) person you might meet here and there, who does the things that we've seen these people do for themselves and others?" We both looked at each other and at exactly the same time, said "It takes a BIKER."

Our friend, John Petrecky, is another example of a man who was always willing to help at every event Dino was involved with, or to help any of his friends for that matter. John would go out of his way to help another biker. We were not surprised to see so many bikes leading the procession to the cemetery on the day of his funeral, despite the cold December weather.

When we visited the Jury Motorcycle Club "Tank" one summer, the event that brought everyone together that day was a benefit to help with expenses for one of their brothers suffering from throat cancer. The Hells Angels one December sponsored a benefit for the children of a local orphanage. The 69ers Motorcycle Club sponsored a "Run for the Animals," donating the desperately needed proceeds to an animal shelter. The Boozefighters held a hunger drive in October and managed to stock the pantry of a local church in Troy that had been empty for weeks prior to that event. One Christmas, the "Boozettes" "adopted" a family and pitched in to buy gifts for a child whose parents were struggling financially. The mother and father cried tears of gratitude as the gifts were presented to them. Another man, Darren Warnken, was killed in a snowmobile accident back in 2001 and for every year since his death, bikers have come together to ride and raise money for Darren's children left behind. These are just a few of the many, many events that bikers are involved in for charity or for someone in need. Anyone who has attended Rolling Thunder in Washington during Memorial Day weekend can attest to the extraordinary efforts of bikers to show their support for veterans every year at that time.

There is great comfort in knowing that my biker friends will be there if I ever need them. The next time I find myself surprised by the actions of a biker or witness the loyalty and devotion of one to his brother, I will be thinking to myself, yes indeed, IT TAKES A BIKER!

~

SEAN
* Intimidating *

"I admire people who treat everyone equally no matter how they look and someone that lives up to their word. A lot of ingredients go into good character."

The first thing I noticed when I met Sean was the 1% diamond pendant around his neck. My eyes then gravitated to his features – long, black hair, stocky, and intimidating. My initial thought was that he didn't look very friendly so I didn't try to make conversation or small talk. Carmella, Dino and I were at the Hillview that day to watch Hank McGrath present the Hells Angels and 69ers Motorcycle Clubs with a Presidential award for Volunteerism. Sean is a member of the 69ers Motorcycle Club North Country Crew. I would see Sean again at various biker events, with or without a shirt under his MC vest (depending on the weather of course), but never without that 1% pendant!

~

"When I was 11 years old, I rented my friend's motorcycle, a Suzuki RM 50cc, for a week..."

Sean grew up in Colonie, New York, with two brothers, and attended parochial school from Kindergarten through sixth grade, then military school from seventh through ninth grade.

His fondest memory of military school was belonging to a rifle team and shooting his 22 rifle at NRA targets in the basement of the school everyday.   Sean finally graduated from a public high school in the Spring of 1986. Sean was the typical mischievous boy, experimenting with nearly impossible jumps on the small bikes he rode when he was young in West Albany. Sean admits to stealing his younger brother's motorcycle in the early days in high school, and remembers riding the bike "until things started falling apart." He would finally notice that it needed to be fixed! The last bike his brother had was a Suzuki DR 200 dirt bike. He convinced his parents to help him purchase a Yamaha MX80 dirt bike when he was 13. He rode that for awhile until life got in the way and he went away to college. Following graduation, Sean spent seven years in different colleges, graduating with a Bachelors of Science degree in Mechanical Engineering. Sean now works as a Senior Draftsman and designs mechanical turbine parts for a large power generation company.

~

"I rode the MX 80 Yamaha dirt bike motorcycle until I blew it up, then afterwards I got a BW 200 Yamaha. I rode that for awhile until I sold it to help buy my first car. Then my younger brother got a DR 200. During that time we moved to an area in Latham where we had hundreds of acres of open fields and woods out back. That's when I started borrowing his bike until I busted the rear rim and sprocket all to hell. I helped him fix it but he forbade me to ride it ever again. That's when I started borrowing the bike without his permission while he was in school."

Sean went right to work after college, skipping his graduation ceremony to begin his career and start making money as soon as possible. *"When I got my first paycheck I started saving for a new Harley-Davidson. That was my dream bike."* He was able to put a $500 deposit down and ordered a motorcycle from Brunswick Harley-Davidson in the Fall of 1993. On March 25, 1994, Sean took delivery of his Harley, a 1994 red Fatboy. The bike would stay with him for eight years until he commissioned a local bike builder to build him a custom-designed chopper.

Those years of education served him well since it was from that background and experience that the concept of "Christine" was born.

Sean told me the hardest part about transitioning from a dirt bike to a Harley was having to stop at red lights! Naturally, since most of his experience before that was off-road, he never had to follow any rules of the road, so learning how to stop for lights and stop signs took some getting used to. These days, Sean owns two bikes: a 2008 Fatbob which he refers to as his "breakdown bike," which he rides when he doesn't take Christine out on the road. I thought it was really interesting when Sean told me that riding his beloved chopper is like driving a Cadillac and that the Fatbob feels like a mini-bike. I usually hear guys tell me the opposite!

"Christine" was named from Stephen King's novel, when after turning the bike off one day, she continued to run for an unusual amount of time! Adding to the mystery of Christine, Sean has had a few mishaps since he's had her on the road, and though the bike needed some minor repairs, Christine was always restored to her original luster, almost as if the bike healed itself. Sean, by the way, does his own mechanical work when he can and told me that if there is ever another bike in his future, he will be the one to build it. Christine has won a few awards in its lifetime, one for "Best Chopper" and other awards at motorcycle shows.

~

"I couldn't believe how easily an innocent person could lose everything"

Sean realized the justice system was not an unbiased system when he witnessed a fellow club member being persecuted by the media for his trouble with the law. The incident made him wary of a judicial system. In the eyes of the judicial system, you're guilty until you can prove your innocence. He saw that a man had to lose everything in order to bail himself out and hire an experienced attorney to convince a jury of his innocence. The whole biker community and friends helped raise money to support his defense.

~

"The only thing that scares me is the thought of crashing on the bike and becoming paralyzed or terminally ill, not able to work and provide for my family, and losing everything."

Everyone who rides a motorcycle knowingly takes their life into their own hands but we do this willingly for the chance to feel the freedom that only comes when you take a bike out on the open road. Still, most bikers, despite the constant threat of accidents, choose to accept the risk in exchange for that liberty.

It's easy to understand why Sean loves the movie, "Braveheart." He admired how the Scottish, being underdogs, fought against the mighty English.

~

"Ever since I was 10 years old, all I wanted for Christmas was tools. No clothes, no toys, just tools!"

No wonder he's so good at his chosen profession, as it was a natural progression to become an engineer with his logical mind and mechanical ability. Today, Sean works as much as possible to take care of his family. Somehow I suspect that Sean is unable to sit idle for long.

~

"It's the law of nature, my parents had all boys so I ended up with a girl."

Sean was devastated when he lost his mother, only 61 years old, due to complications of diabetes. He was very close to his mom and lost his best friend and confidant. Sean's father is still alive and although he doesn't see him often, he talks to him and his brothers on a regular basis. His older brother Mark, 46, is a state attorney and his younger brother, Joe, 41, is a school teacher in Charlotte, North Carolina. The family reunites on holidays, Joe less often because of the distance. Both brothers were also blessed with daughters. His parents instilled in him a strong work ethic. His father was an electrician and always worked hard and his mother, after raising him and his brothers, went to nursing school, then worked at Eden Park Nursing Home in Albany, New York. Sean remembers attending military school at the same time his mother was attending Maria College in Albany.

~

"I almost cried out in joy!"

Sean is a handsome man and has had his share of relationships. When Leah came into his life in October of 2010, Sean fell in love at first sight ("I loved her eyes"), and for the first time felt that this was the woman he would share his life with. Sean and Leah were married on April 23, 2011, and welcomed their first child, Shaylynn, on January 17, 2012. Sean could not describe his feelings when he held his daughter for the first time – "I almost cried out in joy." Leah was raised in New Jersey and wondered in the beginning why such a good-looking guy couldn't find a woman closer to his hometown. The answer is obvious to those who know this couple. Sean and Leah are two very unique individuals but they both think very much alike. It was fate that brought them together. Sean and Leah now live with their baby daughter in Schenectady, New York. Leah describes Sean as an excellent father, although Sean says it's too early for him to judge himself. One thing he IS sure of is that he wants to put his daughter through college and see her become an independent woman. He has seen too many guys take advantage of women who rely on the paychecks of their "deadbeat" boyfriends. Sean is able to provide a stable home for his child and he will be there for her whenever she needs him.

~

"I was raised Catholic but now consider myself more of an Atheist. If worshiping some guy like Jesus makes the general public happy and obedient, with love and respect for others, then so be it. Just don't make it a crime for people who choose to do good without the crutch of some supreme being. It's a shame that it will probably take the general public another hundred years before they finally figure out that they were worshipping a false god."

As a mechanical engineer with a scientific mind, Sean strongly believes that the ancient medieval European governments fabricated organized religion, including the Bible and its Commandments, to breed morality into its societies in order to restore law and order. He believes that the government enacted such beliefs to prevent chaos.

.   Although I am a Catholic and in fact, have been a Catechist for over 10 years, I respect the beliefs of others. Sean's statement caught me a little off-guard but as I thought about it, I began to understand how and why he may have come to believe that the world's major religions are in fact man-made. The problems with the various crises in the Catholic Church during the past 10 years have resulted in a falling away of many previously devout Catholics. Our trust was irrevocably breached and for many there is no recovery. Interestingly though, Sean and Leah still intend to raise their child to be a "God-fearing individual." In years to come, Shaylynn may bring him back to the Church, or she will choose a path similar to her father's.

~

"I enjoy being around other hardcore motorcycle enthusiasts who love motorcycles and ride every chance they get."

Sean joined a club for the brotherhood that is paramount among club members. He wakes up every day and reads the motorcycle catalogs and magazines while most people are reading the newspaper. He loves the camaraderie that comes with fellow bikers and he prefers to ride in small groups with a defined destination. Sean enjoys the ride more when he has a planned destination. There is a little more safety in numbers since it's impossible not to see or hear a pack of bikers rumbling nearby. While Sean loves sharing the ride with his brothers, he still maintains his autonomous nature.

Sean values his friends and club brothers and has always chosen to give others the benefit of the doubt, instead of judging people on the surface. He believes that wisdom comes from a combination of life experience and learning from suffering and surviving. Sean has experienced situations that have taught him how quickly and easily our freedom can be taken away and because of this he appreciates the power of biker brotherhood even more.

~

"I love riding fast, if you're not riding at 100 mph then you are taking up too much space. I'm a hardcore motorcycle enthusiast who loves the actual sport of

motorcycling - leaning into turns, hearing the steady beat
of the motor while the wind is hitting my face. I put up
with bad weather in order to squeeze out a ride on days
that are questionable."

You are more open to the elements on a bike, you see more, hear more. Sean loves the actual sport of riding – leaning into turns, hearing the steady beat of the motor. His favorite moments are when he is riding into the "S" turns and finds himself upon a series of barns and yards. A stranger's backyard becomes an intriguing landscape as you gaze upon it from the seat of a motorcycle. Rolling hills and blue skies depict a scene of tranquility. No wonder Sean says much of his time on the bike is spent relaxing and thinking about life. Some kind of magical transformation comes over mind and body as you feel at one with the machine. Sean will tend to explore more when he's riding his motorcycle as opposed to his truck. Those unfamiliar back roads which he will avoid in the truck become an exciting adventure to pursue on the bike.

Sean mentioned a few of the most memorable rides he's had, one in particular when he was riding out a storm from Utica to Albany. After riding 45 minutes through the pouring rain, suddenly within seconds the sky opened up, the sun was shining and enveloped him like a warm blanket (which he desperately needed after being soaked to the bone)! Another memorable moment for him was riding his brand new 2008 HD Fatbob up to the top of the hill climb behind Sporty's in Minerva and back down without a scratch - just for the hell of it.

~

"I would like to travel and see the rest of the world,
especially Devil's Tower, Mt. Rushmore, Red Rocks,
the Natural Land Bridge..."

Sean plans to travel much more in the future, on the motorcycle and off. He would like to "walk down the street and see how other people live." Sean remembers a few summers at the beach in New Jersey and plans to visit the beach often with his wife and daughter.

In the years I have known Sean as an acquaintance, then as a friend, I have found him to be a serious, honorable man with a fearless intensity, further strengthened by his brothers and those he treasures.

~

"For the strength of the pack is the Wolf and the strength of the Wolf is the pack"...Rudyard Kipling

SEAN

* HARDCORE BADASS BIKERS *

~

When someone refers to a biker as being "hardcore," what does it mean? Does it mean that the guy is bad to the bone, rough, tough, mean, and has no soul? If hardcore also means "badass," what would the opposite be – a goodass? There are misconceptions galore in the biker subculture and labels are abundant.

Hardcore doesn't have to be synonymous with motorcycle club member or one-percenter. Club members are as varied as the collection of people you see at the grocery store every day. Big, tall, short, round, bearded, bald, tattooed or pierced, you name it, bikers include all types.

Hardcore may mean the man is a long-time biker, someone who has "grown up" in the lifestyle of a nomad, perhaps estranged or abandoned by their family (or maybe by choice). He could be someone who simply learned at an early age that he loves riding a motorcycle more than anything else in his life and prefers to live and breathe with others who share his passion. There are many hardcore bikers in this area and though a few may wear the mask of a devil, their hearts hold more love and respect for their brothers than most people realize.

Hardcore does imply the man has a tough interior (hard to the core) but more often than not, the term describes the man's personal principles rather than any matters of the heart and soul. He does not back away from confrontations and will not hesitate to fight viciously for something or someone he loves. Intimidation is foreign to him. His independence from restriction and conformity are fiercely protected. If he wants to wear jeans and a leather jacket to church, he will do so proudly. He believes in freedom and knows the value of liberty and justice for all. If that is a true description of a badass, then that is the kind of person with which this author would choose to be surrounded. The United States of America is a free country and there is always room for diversity. Whatever cause or whoever you choose to ally yourself with is your choice. After all, someone's got to support the goodasses too.

~

* NEVER JUDGE A COVER *

~

Since I have been involved with bikers and *New York Rider Magazine*, there are many things I've learned that have shattered every perception I ever held true in my mind regarding bikers, outlaw and otherwise.

As a child, I would watch the bikers ride by and wish I was one of them, but at the same time I was intimidated by their presence. The intimidation factor is also part of the attraction for me. Naturally, I thought those guys were tougher, more street-smart, rough (in and around the edges), big, burly, unfriendly, and most likely all working as mechanics or at gas stations around the world. Dear readers, I have graduated from being totally intimidated to feeling totally comfortable around bikers. Years ago, I would never have considered approaching a biker to make conversation or walking into a biker bar on my own, now I actually prefer biker bars over other bars, and of course the company of bikers around me has somehow become a requirement for me to be content these days.

Perception – Bikers are rough, tough, and mean!
Rough? There may be some truth to this perception, but it is really a matter of opinion. Whatever makes a person rough and tough may actually be just a personality trait. Sure, the black leather makes anyone look a little tough (and yes, it really does make us feel tough), in fact, wearing black all the time does seem to send some kind of signal to society that you are in cahoots with "the dark side," but it's really all just part of the subculture. It's our way of categorizing ourselves into a special "club" that is actually another small world within our own universe. It feels good too when we meet up with people so compatible with us, others who feel exactly the same way we do about riding and why we love it. It's like meeting your match over and over again and sharing the fires that spark!

Tough? Maybe, but I have found more often that the toughness is revealed only when necessary. Bikers can be defensive creatures, mostly out of habit since it goes with the territory on the road, after all. Of course a biker will always be ready for the unexpected, including conflicts, and I have yet to meet a biker who will not fight fiercely for his beliefs. Resilient, though, is a better adverb for bikers. Try to find a biker who has survived a crash and spends the rest of his life wallowing in pity. He will do everything in his power to get back on his bike and live his life with pride and dignity. Against all odds, his heart continues to beat fast and furiously for freedom in the wind.

Mean? This perception couldn't be further from the truth. Over and over I have been proven wrong on the rare occasions that I've let myself judge a man by the length of his beard or how grungy he appears. In fact, contrary to what I might originally think, I find these men so endearing after talking awhile, that I start to see the messy hair and worn-out jeans as a costume that someone might don for a special occasion, only in this case, the costume becomes part of the essence that sets them apart. I love the unspoken biker attitude of "take me as I am," with no need to impress each other, no need to boast of their latest business deal or how much money they made this year. All of that information is irrelevant. Bikers seek and usually find the person "under the surface." Why? Maybe because every biker knows that he/she is gambling every time they hop on the bike. We know we are more vulnerable to the elements, to accidents, and we appreciate our time together that much more. For these same reasons, most of us embrace each other upon meeting and bidding farewell. Bikers cut through the everyday, mundane issues that plague all of us, at least during the ride, because we know the passage of time is so inevitable. We want to *know* each other *now,* and to do that we must be *real.* Bikers are some of the most honest, hard-working, and loyal people you will ever meet if you are lucky enough. Honorable people, and far, far from mean.

Perception: Bikers are all mechanics or gas station attendants!
First, there is absolutely nothing wrong with mechanics or gas-station attendants. This is only an example of what *I* preconceived in *my* mind about bikers (just as someone might assume I was a professional writer). Imagine my surprise to learn that after meeting hundreds of bikers, I still haven't met one who works as a mechanic or gas-station attendant! Instead, I know biker doctors, biker lawyers, biker cops, biker truck drivers, biker office workers, you get the idea. Here's an analogy:

bikers are like ice cream – they come in all different flavors and varieties – small, medium, large, hard, soft, low-fat, high-fat, and their occupations follow suit. In the biker world, you never know whether you're talking to a convenience store clerk or a rocket scientist.

Perception: Bikers have no heart!

Newsflash: Bikers have bigger hearts than most people. Consider that they spend a lot of their time on weekends attending charity functions (READ 'contributing money to charities'), and the other part of their week either at their daily occupation, helping a brother or sister, or visiting someone in a hospital, and maybe you will realize the truth of this revelation. The most wonderful people who work for Hospice in Albany, New York, are biker friends of ours (has anyone ever met people with more compassion than Hospice angels?), and not only "introduced" us to the "Rolling Thunder Ride to the Wall," but watched over Dino and I on our first trip down to Washington, always making sure we stayed with the pack and didn't fall behind. I cannot begin to count the many bikers, men and women, who at first struck me as rough around the edges and unapproachable, only to learn fairly quickly that I was so utterly mistaken. It's not as though they are trying to hide their hearts, rather, I believe it is the public's eternal perception that bikers are cold, heartless people who only want to cause all kinds of trouble, make lots of noise, and wreck havoc on everyone's lives. This was the one perception I was absolutely delighted to have shattered. Still, so many times I invite friends of mine who are not bikers to attend a biker event and they always have some excuse not to go, or they tell me they would never "fit in." This is so ironic. If there is any arena in this world where you don't have to worry about "fitting in," it is undoubtedly a public biker event. I have seen all ages, all sizes, and all colors at biker events. There is no end to the diversity you will see, among those brave souls who do venture out into the biker community for a few hours. It's like a whole village of people standing in the direct path of a rainbow.

Perception: They're all gang members and they only hang out with their own kind!

One of the very first lessons I learned was to never, never, never refer to a biker, especially one who is also a club member, as a *gang* member. Bikers do know the difference between the word "club" and "gang" and definitely do not care to be charged with having a gang mentality. Any links that people see between gangs and biker clubs are totally off base. Bikers are not "West Side Story" wannabes looking for a rumble on every corner. Club members are people who choose to join and belong to a particular club (or brotherhood, or "family"), like-minded individuals with their own talents to bring to the family. They are like branches on a tree, together they make up a strong united force and when one breaks, the others feel the pain. Gangs, on the other hand, are usually more inclined toward inciting violence and perpetuating that reputation. Of course there are criminal elements in every society. I do not believe there are more or less in the biker subculture. Human nature does not change, whether you're a biker club member or a librarian. We are all vulnerable to crime and our own temperament determines our reactions. While it may be true that bikers tend to hang out with their own kind more often than not, and that would be a normal, instinctive thing to do, it is not true that bikers segregate themselves from non-bikers. Remember, opposites attract, and there are many biker couples who are not really biker couples! The husband might ride but the wife may be terrified to ever get on a Harley. The wife may be a "woman in the wind" but her husband might be content to spend his weekends playing golf.

Perception: They all have long hair, tattoos, and piercings!
Many bikers do have long hair, tattoos and piercings, and it does make for a colorful mix. But there are some who will never be tattooed, like to wear their hair in crew cuts and despise piercings of any kind. All of these elements, however, make a statement. It can be some sort of declaration or just a glimpse into a person's soul. We all express ourselves in different ways. My ways happen to be through writing and music. My husband's is through photography. Yes, many of our friends choose to talk through their tattoos. Finding your own passion is absolutely essential in this life.

*Never judge a person by their cover. Take some time now
and then to lift your own veil and
peek under the masks you see!*

~

TIM ABARE
* Survivor *

*"I love to ride because I spend so much time in my
own head, it is more peaceful. I always thought the
mythological Centurion was cool and I loved the solidarity
between body/mind and movement in that creature,
almost like the bike is the bottom half of my body!"*

I met Tim through my association with *New York Rider
Magazine.* Tim wrote an article about himself and asked me
to review and edit. I edited his article and he hated my editing!
So I opted to print the article the way it was originally written,
with misspellings, bad grammar and all, rather than make an
issue out of the matter since I hadn't met Tim in person yet and
knew next to nothing about him. He eventually apologized to me
and I accepted of course (never could resist an apology from a
handsome biker). We finally met in person at a charity bike run
in the summer of 2008 and have been friends ever since.

My first impression of Tim was that he was one of those
tough, macho guys who are over-confident and used to getting
everything they want. Anyone who knows Tim knows his bike
too, aptly titled, "Flamethrower," because Tim likes to shoot the
flames out of the back tailpipe at every event he attends. This
causes quite a stir among the many bystanders and you can
see that Tim clearly enjoys the thrill of it all. Tim is tall, about

6'1", extremely handsome, looks great in leather and Levis, and carries himself well. I learned over time, however, that there was a lot more to Mr. Abare than meets the eye.

~

"I was 14 years old when I took my first ride on my cousin's Harley Sportster. I knew that was it. My first project bike was a Honda 250 R 3-wheeler, which I bought off of a guy in a McDonald's parking lot for $750. It had a clutch and a thumb throttle and I thought, " What the hell am I going to do with this?" Well, I swapped the throttle to the left and used some PVC to work the clutch, put it in gear, and was on my way!"

Tim has the use of only one arm. His right arm was paralyzed from a motorcycle accident when he was younger. As a result, he lost the use of his right arm. Tim wears his right arm in a sling due to permanent nerve damage and chooses not to live through the painful process of amputation and prosthesis. Years of wearing the sling have brought Tim to actually look natural with it and his many friends don't even notice it anymore. Oh, did I mention that Tim rides with ape hangers and handles them with expert efficiency? This is a characteristic of Tim that people usually find quite amazing and a little disconcerting. Most of us can't figure out how or why he handles a bike with ape hangers, considering his handicap, and how the hell he does it so well!

Tim remembers the day of the accident that changed his life. He was drinking and riding (never a good idea) his Honda 1100F, traveling at excessive speed.

~

"It was June 9, 1985. I was fooling around on a Honda, passed a car towing a boat. In front of the car was a truck with a camper. The car swerved to get out of the way and the camper caught my right side. I went flipping through the air and came down on my head and shoulder. And the nerves went pop, pop, pop. Two cars behind me, an RN and old friend, Martha Siver, got out of a car. I kept saying, "Take me to my mom's I'll be aright in the morning." I almost lost my leg, docs operated for 13 hours."

Tim's mother, Nancy Morgia, was asked if his chest was deformed as a result of the accident, as it seemed bloated. His mom told the nurses there was no chest deformity but it appeared that way because Tim was bleeding internally. The medical team operated on Tim, cutting through his clavicle and splicing the artery, finally succeeding in starting the blood pumping. Unfortunately, as the blood pumped, it clotted and those blood clots were forced to the end of his fingers, causing Tim to lose those fingertips. His prognosis was dire, and he was told that he would probably never walk again. The damage to his arm was irreversible, nerve endings were severed. Tim credits the doctor on call that night, Dr. Richard Worthington, his mother's high school friend, with saving his life. Upon waking in the hospital Tim heard his stepfather's voice telling him that he could not move his arm. Ten days later, his parents arranged for him to be sent to the Humana Arm & Hand Clinic in Louisville, Kentucky. Dr. Peacock would be caring for him there, along with four other surgeons.

Dr. Peacock's plan was to cut the back of Tim's leg and attempt to re-run a nerve tube from his leg to his arm with the hope that new nerves would grow in the arm. Preparations were made for Tim to have surgery the next morning. Following a battery of tests, it was determined that nerves were pulled from his spine, not his arm, and were also causing his eye to droop. This discovery meant there was nothing the doctors could do. Tim was actually relieved because he didn't want to be cut up (*"All the science fiction stuff freaked me out"*). Tim returned to Watertown that summer. It was a long time before he got back on a motorcycle, in large part due to not knowing how to customize a bike one-handed and live with a handicap, and also because of his stepfather's attitude toward motorcycles. His stepfather never liked motorcycles and on one Mother's Day told him to take the helmet with all the stickers and go (since the nieces and nephews were getting old enough to read).

~

"In the biker world, this isn't a handicap; instead, it's almost like an "Attaboy!" There is no judgment in the biker world."

Tim bought a house in Henderson, and on St. Patrick's Day, lived through his second major accident. He was leaving a wedding and while driving home, fell asleep in the truck, veered off the road, rolled the truck and was thrown out, landing in a ditch, and breaking his neck and leg.

~

"I remember lying in the grass, feeling the cold, wet, dewy grass on my face. I could hear cars driving past me. Someone stopped, then left... apparently went back to the bar that she worked at and got help. As I laid there in the ditch, the cops asked if I had been drinking. My neck was broken and my right leg had to be casted all the way down to my toes."

Tim's trouble on the road continued when he decided to ride his Heritage to Alexandria Bay, New York, on July 2, 2000. He was pulled over for speeding by 13 cops - the State police, park police, sheriff, and border patrol! He was arrested for Driving While Intoxicated (DWI) and had to call a cab to get back to his truck at Sackett's Harbor. During the second week in July, he attended a pig roast in Mexico, New York, for "Branded Ones." Riding back to Henderson, he hit a deer straight on. The deer blew up, Tim was thrown from the bike, rolling over the road, and although suffering skin burns, and covered with blood, he got back on the bike and rode back to the bar. The following week in July, Tim was out at Willy's Bar in Dexter, New York, had a few shots (*"I don't do shots.."*), left in his truck, with no brakes, hit a curb and popped a tire. He kept driving, shredded his tire, cutting his brake lines, and brushed another vehicle. Tim got out and walked home through the woods. Of course the police were called and Tim was found hiding out like a fugitive, in Sackett's. He was arrested for DWI and his family and friends were thinking and hoping that this might possibly be the end of Tim's biker days. That did not prove to be the case!

~

"Sure, I did drugs (smoked pot and tried other stuff) when I thought they were "in." It was acceptable and contributed to the tough guy image."

Tim never knew his biological father. His mother married young and was pregnant for Tim when Tim's father died. Tim's mom used to tell him that he was born a hundred years too late and should have been a mountain man! His father, Tony Abare, used to race hydro boats and while being flown over his course for the next day on June 9, 1961, the plane crashed and he was killed. Tim was born the following December. His mother remarried and Tim was brought up Italian but is actually French and Welsh.

~

**"I was raised Catholic but no longer believe in the
fictional characteristic of God that we grew up with.
That is a myth."**

Tim speaks of his family with great affection. He has one brother, Nicky, and four sisters, Toni, Teri, Lisa, and Wendy. Tim is close to all of them, and loves spending time with his nieces and nephews. He admires his siblings and their family values, and envies the lives they've built for themselves. Teaching seems to be a genetic trait in Tim's family, as all of Tim's siblings are teachers of Physical Education, Health, and Spanish. He is especially proud of his brother, Nicky, who, after a career as a Biology teacher, decided to become a New York State Trooper! His sister, Wendy, married a high school friend, and Tim remembers that when a close uncle died, Wendy "stepped up" to take care of the rest of the family (she was there for my dad). The relatives on the Abare side take turns planning family reunions, usually held every five years. Tim's grandmother, the matriarch of the family, who lives in Watertown, is 104 years old! She loves hearing his biker stories and always asks him if he's been on "any of those road rides lately."

Tim loves the movie, "Jeremiah Johnson," with Robert Redford, because he likes the idea of a strong individual forced to survive as a mountain man, isolated from the rest of the world. However, Tim is content with the accomplishments he's made with his life's work. He has been an employee of National Grid for 26 years, holding various positions within the company. If all goes well, he should retire with a modest salary and reap the benefits of his long career.

~

***"I went to college for one semester and passed with a 4.0,
receiving an Oxytology Certificate from Seagrams."***

Tim always planned to marry and raise children, however,
for whatever reason, so far, those stars have not crossed for
him. One of the saddest things in life is to long for something or
someone and never have that yearning satisfied. I do believe,
though, and I hope Tim does, that nothing is impossible and
someday he will find his princess in shining leathers, and he will
become a father. Tim would treasure those gifts. If fate does not
allow this, then maybe his loneliness will be assuaged in other
ways. His compassion has suffered no deficit from being denied
fatherhood. He knows how to love unconditionally.

Although he is a bit cynical after being hurt so many times and
in his opinion, has repeatedly failed at maintaining committed
relationships, a light still shines in his eyes with the hope that
his search for total happiness will prove fruitful. Taking chances
is something Tim will never shy away from.

~

***"I've been in love three times, but I've never been able to
figure out why I am not able to maintain a functional
relationship. I've always wanted to get married and have
kids. That is my only regret."***

Tim has had his share of women and heartache and this is
how I learned more about the inside of Tim. While going through
a sad and unexpected breakup with a woman, Tim turned to me
one day to ask my opinion on the situation since I knew both
of them and had spent time with them together. Our talking
and listening relationship began there and eventually developed
into a special friendship that to me was so far from what I ever
thought it would be. I am usually intimidated by guys like Tim.
I am attracted to that macho, over-confident quality but am
also afraid of it. Maybe I'm afraid that I won't be worthy of the
macho man's attention, who knows (and that will be another
book someday)! Nevertheless, we get along very well, at least
emotionally and intellectually, because we discovered that we
had similar feelings and attitudes about life and love. Tim
learned that I wasn't just Dino's wife and someone who writes for

a magazine, and I learned that Tim's heart was so much bigger than his perceived macho-ness. The key word is perceived. My perception about him was way off. I find him to be intense in an emotional way and I don't mean that to sound like a weakness; on the contrary, I think it can be a huge strength. Tim loves with his whole being. We all wish for that kind of person to be close to, someone who loves you so passionately that you feel it just by being in their presence. I know this is true about him because I have witnessed him in love. I felt his pain when he spoke of the loss he felt; he was truly grieving for the closeness he had with that person, and somehow he communicated that to me without sounding like a poor, lost puppy. I'm guessing that for him it was more akin to feeling as if a part of him was drifting away while he was desperately struggling not to fall into the black hole of depression.

~

"I don't see in me what other people see."

Tim has many friends and when he is in the mood, he is quite the social spirit. He will participate in motorcycle events if he feels it will benefit a worthy cause, and he never tires of entertaining an audience with his flame-throwing talents. Despite his physical and emotional scars, Tim is a strong man with a noble character. Honesty and integrity are important to him and he is wise beyond his years. He will absorb himself completely for a friend in need, and can be trusted to weather any storm alongside those for whom he cares deeply. Tim's heart is huge and his capacity to love is endless. He is a proud man who harbors no ill will toward others. He would rather share the blame and carry the burden than to inflict more pain or seek revenge. He knows there is no justice when hearts are broken.

~

"I believe wisdom comes from age and experience. I don't judge people but I do beat myself up sometimes. I have a high level of integrity, I'm "old school" – I will help any person in need."

A very sobering time in Tim's life was the year his dogs died. Tim lived with five dogs in an old farmhouse in the country.

During one extremely cold winter, he stayed at his parents for a couple of weeks. His stepfather advised him to pour antifreeze into the toilets at the farmhouse to keep the pipes from freezing. Unfortunately, while Tim was away, two of his dogs drank out of the toilet and died from ingesting the antifreeze. Trapper, a 120 lb. Black Lab, was his best friend. HeavyD was the other. He lost the other two dogs, Papa and Mozie, from old age.

~

"I would really love to see live whales and wild mustangs. I do have a desire to travel, but I can't imagine not being on my bike. I plan to ride to Sturgis someday."

I have always admired Tim for his courage in accepting his plight in life and dealing with his handicap without inviting sympathy from those around him. He is a true gentleman and respectful which is probably why he is able to maintain close friendships with women. I think he knows how to tune into a person's thoughts and listen intently, a talent that only comes from being able to step outside of your own mind for awhile, even if it might bring you out of your comfort zone.

~

"Do what you can with what you have where you are."
Theodore Roosevelt

Regardless of what the future holds for Tim, he will survive and I know he will continue to touch the lives of everyone he meets. Despite the tragic misfortunes and whatever faults he feels he has himself that contribute or lead to the destruction of his romantic relationships, a certain strength comes through, a strength coupled with the hope and belief that someday things *will* get better, even if there's yet another mountain this man must conquer.

~

"Neither a borrower nor a lender be; For loan oft loses both itself and friend, And borrowing dulls the edge of husbandry. This above all: to thine own self be true, And it must follow, as the night the day, Thou canst not then be false to any man.

Farewell: my blessing season this in thee!"

William Shakespeare

TIM ABARE

* MUSIC TO YOUR EARS *

~

When you walk by a Cathedral at just the right moment, you may hear the sound of the bell from the bell tower....or you may not. For some, the sound just becomes part of the background noise of everyday life. Until recently, that is. While walking to my parking garage one day, for some reason I was stopped in my tracks because amid all the other sounds around me, such as traffic, people talking, birds, etc., a particular melody wafted through the sound of the bell. "What a sweet melody for a Tuesday afternoon," was the first thought in my mind, followed by the question, "Who is tolling that bell?" Looking around at the people surrounding me, it seemed apparent that no one else was hearing the bell. This little incident in the middle of my day conjured up all kinds of thoughts about the bell-ringer, such as whether it was a male or female, and how he/she must love making this kind of music, knowing that most people are not listening!

Rap music is noise to my ears and is largely ignored or unnoticed by me. It just does not reach me in any way (apologies to all the rap lovers out there). On the other hand, a Puccini aria from one of his operas will bring me to tears, and an old Aerosmith tune from the 1970's will take me back to my teenage years and have me re-living all kinds of memories. Sound, noise, and music touches us in very individual ways.

There are many for whom the sound of a motorcycle is too loud, deafening, and simply an ugly noise to be endured every once in awhile. But to bikers, the sound of a motorcycle engine is beautiful music to our ears. The rumble of the motor, and especially if there is more than one, triggers a sense of exciting anticipation, almost like an adrenaline rush, making you feel like hopping on a bike and following the pack, wherever they may lead. Just as rap music does nothing for me, there are apparently enough fans to propel rap singers to fortune and fame. The bell-ringer continues to toll his bell for those few who appreciate the resonating sound echoing from the air. And for those who find the sound of motorcycles a dreaded blast to be tolerated, there may be twice as many who savor the music that only a motorcycle can create. Ride safe, listen, and find your own music.

~

* TOGETHER WITH MY LEATHER *

~

Have you ever wondered why and how bikers became synonymous with leather? Well, the old timers might tell us it's all about protection, but I think it's probably 50% protection and 50% fashion statement. You bikers can't stand before me looking cool in your black leather and tell me all that coolness is due to your need for protection.

Bikers wear lots of leather – boots, chaps, gloves, chain wallets, and of course the leather jacket. By the way, I always thought the chain wallets were purely for a "badass" look. Imagine my surprise to learn that there really is a purpose for the chain! Since motorcycles vibrate, which places stress on the back pocket, the wallet can drop out unnoticed and lost and with the chain, this won't happen. I don't know why I never thought of that, it just never occurred to me while admiring a Harley man's wallet and chain. I was surprised to learn that the earliest jackets connected to bikers were from 1920-1930. These jackets copied the A-1 jacket used by the Army Air Corps prior to WWII, made from thick horsehide because hides were abundant during that time. Those thick hides do provide protection from weather and can reduce levels of injury. Riding in cool weather gets very cold when you are moving at 55 miles per hour. Chaps, which are worn over normal pants/jeans, are an invaluable shield from cold and wind. The last thing you want is to be freezing your butt off while out on a 300-mile ride. That takes a lot of the fun out of riding! A wise biker will also dress to protect him/herself from a potential fall. You may have to drop a bike to avoid being hit by a car, experience a blowout or lose control (and even the most experienced rider can drop a bike).

The Schott Company, opened in 1913 in NYC, began producing motorcycle jackets during the 1920's. Other early jacket retailers include Indian and Harley-Davidson. Harley, apparently, makes a damn good leather jacket, and the 1940's Cycle Champ and Cycle Queen Harley-Davidson design defined the style and function of the leather jacket. Then there was Marlon Brando's influence in "The Wild Ones," in which his double-breasted Schott jacket became the norm.

Leather gloves are an item that I can't get enough of, with at least five or six pairs in my possession. I see a style I love and I have to buy them. I don't know what it is, I just love leather gloves. They also make holding handlebars for hours more comfortable. Touring gloves will have additional features such as reinforced palms, insulating material, and waterproof fabric. Gloves come in different weights for different seasons. Summer gloves are naturally thinner and lighter without any lining. Fingerless gloves are ok but if you're riding in extreme sunny/ hot conditions, perforations in gloves can cause a sunburn. Most people settle on medium weight gloves which can be used for any season. There are thicker gloves made for cold weather. It's worth the extra money to get a pair of gloves that are water-resistant, and insulation will help when the wind starts creeping into the stitches of the fingertips.

Boots are another must-have item for bikers. A good pair of boots can make the difference when trying to avoid dropping a bike. It is much harder to steady yourself and your bike with thin-bottom shoes.   Boots also provide protection from hot exhaust pipes and support the ankles when getting on and off the bike. I burned more than one pair of boots on hot pipes, and it's a good thing I was wearing boots, even though they were ruined (those boots saved my "feetsies")! When you shop around for your boots, make sure they grip the ankle and heel and that they are water-resistant. Boots that include a heel under the sole will make it easier to rest on the foot pegs and will provide a good grip in mud, water, sand, and oil, should you need such a grip. A great pair of boots can be found at general shoe stores, so you need not spend a fortune for a good pair.

Now let's talk about the leather jacket. Your jacket should fit a bit looser than a non-leather jacket so that you'll be able to wear something under it on cold days. Arms need longer sleeves, shoulders need more space, lower back needs more material, jacket needs to contain closings to keep out wind and rain. The more pockets, the better, with at least one inner pocket (preferably waterproof). I remember riding one day and being very thankful for my many pockets. Not being able to carry a huge handbag in the bike, I needed pockets for a camera (so I could take pictures while riding), my sunglasses, etc., and realized then the value of a well-designed biker jacket. Outer pockets, however, are useless if they can't be closed. You will need a jacket with a good, strong zipper, and even better if the zipper has a cover-up because wind blows through zipper teeth. The zipper cover will make your jacket much warmer on cold, windy days. If you are in the market for a heavy-duty leather jacket, extra padding in essential places (elbows, shoulders and back) is mandatory. There are even motorcycle jackets that use an airbag system, which deploys in the event of an accident, inflating to protect the rider's neck, torso, and lower back (all I can think of is the Michelin Man). Also important is reflective material on the jacket because the number one reason for motorcycle accidents is that another driver did not see you. A good leather jacket may be expensive but worth it.

Leather is a material made from tanned animal hides, and has actually been used as clothing since the earliest days of human existence. Leather shoes were found in the tombs of Egyptian pharaohs! Following is some of the information I read about the leather tanning process on Answers.com: "Antelope, buckskin, lambskin, sheepskin, and cowhide are the hides most commonly used to make leather jackets. As soon as the skin is removed from the animal at the meat processing plant, it is refrigerated, salted, or packed in barrels of brine. It is then sent to the tannery where the skins undergo a series of processes designed to preserve and soften the hides." The leather will undergo one of three types of tanning: vegetable, mineral, or oil tanning. Vegetable tanning involves soaking the animal skin in stronger tannic acid for several weeks, but some soft leathers may be soaked for as little as 12 hours. Mineral tanning is faster but can change the color of the leather. Skins are placed in alum salt-filled drums fitted with paddles that provide a constant agitating motion. The mildest form of tanning is oil tanning, where fish oil is simply sprayed onto the skins. By the way, remember that leather is not waterproof, so if you happen to get caught in the rain (and you will), let your jacket dry slowly, then apply a leather restorer to get the oils back.

After tanning, skins are washed again and wrung out thoroughly. The skins are then passed under a band knife, which cuts the skins to a uniform thickness, then places them on a conveyer belt to be carried to drying tunnels and stretched on frames to prevent shrinkage during the drying stage. The hides are conditioned with water and soap, placed in machines that manipulate the leather so the fibers are made more flexible, and then finally hung once more in vacuum-drying cabinets. While skins are dried they are buffed with revolving steel cylinders covered with abrasive paper. This is when glazes, dyes and lacquers are applied, then sent to the garment factory for designers to create the jacket design. I was surprised to learn how the color is set into a leather jacket and that the way the color is dyed into the jacket has an effect on the quality of the jacket. It can be done in two different ways. One way is to have the dye sprayed into the leather which only goes into the top layer of the leather (so if you scratched it, you would find a different color under). Another way is called a "dye soak," where the leather is soaked and completely covered and of course more expensive.

During the design process, the pattern is placed on top of the leather, and the leather is cut by being placed on moving tables called spreaders. The spreading table works on a conveyer system, moving the fabric to the cutting machine, which is fitted with either rotary blades or band-knives. (Are you surprised yet at what a lengthy process this is?!) The final process of transforming that animal skin into a jacket is "pressing." Pressing involves heat application, steaming, and blocking. Steam and pressure are regulated to give the jacket its shape. Curved blocks are placed around collars and cuffs, heat applied, blocks removed, leaving collars and cuffs curved. Each jacket is inspected by hand before it leaves the factory floor. Jackets are then covered with plastic sheathing, packed into cartons, and shipped to the retailer.

Your leathers have gone through a lot to get to you. I think I have a new respect for my good ol' leather jacket. There will always be something cool about wearing leather - it changes attitudes and breeds confidence. As Nicholas Cage said in "Wild at Heart," A good jacket is 'your symbol of individuality.' **Enjoy the Hide!**

~

Z
* Wisdom *

" I realized that the only thing holding me back in life was me. I was bitter at everyone and felt the world was against me. I realized that the only one against me was me. At that point I knew that I was as good as anybody else and I could do what other people do and do it well."

I first met Z while stranded at an airport in Newark, New Jersey in late October of 2008. My brother and I were on our way home from a trip to Texas and Z and members of his club were traveling back from the Boozefighters Motorcycle Club National meeting in Fort Worth. I was at least familiar with the Boozefighters, as I had recently done a story on the evolution of the biker culture in which the club was included. After introducing myself as the Editor of *New York Rider Magazine*, I asked if he would be willing to be interviewed. Z led me to one of the quieter corners of the airport and we began.

My first impression of Z was intimidation, though not in any kind of dangerous connotation. It was clear to me from the start that he was somehow a "leader" among his club brothers, and very well respected. I quickly learned that Z is the Northeast Representative for the Boozefighters Motorcycle Club as well as the Charter holder of the Mountain Chapter 60. Perhaps it was the manner in which he was regarded by his peers that intimidated me to a certain degree, however, Z, all by himself, seemed to command respect (and an audience).

~

"What drove me into a club was the history about my club and its brotherhood."

Z proceeded to tell me about the rich history and tradition of the Boozefighters MC, their place in the world of motorcycle clubs, and how and why he became involved. Z has been a biker all his life and a BFMC member for 22 years.

The Boozefighters Motorcycle Club Mountain Chapter was established in October of 1996 in the beautiful and historical Catskill Mountain Region of New York. The mission and goal of the Mountain Chapter is to continue the Boozefighters Motorcycle Club's long history and tradition of brotherhood, riding, racing, and partying. Z told me much of this information in his own way, as any good historian and storyteller would. If I asked him something he could not (or would not answer), he would just smile quietly. He made it clear that club business would not be discussed, which I respect and accept. I saw the wisdom in this man's eyes and it was enchanting. I was a captive audience for his accounts of the experiences he's had over the years.

I sometimes think of Z as the "father" of the Mountain Chapter. Even though the club elects their officers, Z serves as the voice of reason and wisdom when called upon. Most if not all of the bikers within our tri-city area (Albany, Schenectady, Troy), and around the world, know Z and know that his years of experience and good judgment have proven him to be an extremely valuable member of the biker community, as well as a force to be reckoned with when necessary.

~

"I graduated from college and studied under an Oxford Scholar, Dr. Carl Rex Stockton, from Oxford University at McKendree University in Lebanon, Illinois. In high school the guidance counselor told me I would be in prison my whole life. He said I would not make it out of school."

~

"What is the real definition of real love?"

Z is married to a wonderful woman named Ellen and is a devoted father of two and a man who learned from experience how important it is to keep God and your family close to your heart. He and Ellen met about 10 years ago at a biker event. When Z shook her hand he couldn't let go, and they have been together ever since! Now retired, Z has worked at several jobs throughout his life and as a result has a very diverse background, as well as hundreds of friends who were former co-workers and acquaintances.

~

"The only regret I have is not learning the skills my father had. I was too busy running the streets. My father was a skilled, talented man. I was too stubborn to be there."

Z's comment about his father surprises me because I have known Z to be a man who appears to be a 'natural' educator, albeit a teacher of life. There have been many instances where Z has acted as teacher, professor, and yes, disciplinarian, in his lifetime. This is obviously what his father taught him, perhaps unknowingly, and which Z came to discover later in life. He uses this unexpected gift from his father to the benefit of everyone around him and most return with gratitude for his invaluable wisdom and advice. Z knows that the best way to resolve differences is to allow input from all parties involved and have the scene play itself out until the final conflict is settled. He will intervene only if absolutely necessary. This is how the concept of "Learn so you may teach" is realized, and most often his "students" will reap from this knowledge at times in their lives when they need it most desperately. Respect is extremely important to Z and one will notice this in the first few moments spent with this man. It is no surprise to me that he lists his favorite movie as *"The Godfather,"* because it is *"all about respect."*

~

"I feel my character is one that is of good insight, good judgment, and one that is fair and is about respect. I am no better than anybody else, nor am I less than anybody else. I am just a pebble on the beach."

Motorcycle club life is very demanding and it takes a person with strong character to survive for any period of time in the biker subculture. There will always be disagreements to be dealt with, unpleasant confrontations, and moments of deep frustration. This is human nature and bikers are not exempt. It is easy to play either the Cowboy or the Indian, and fortunately Z is able to wear both hats, and excels at both roles. His years of living the biker lifestyle and his experiences on both sides of the law, so to speak, have enabled him to retain a unique perspective on life and human relationships. Yet Z in all his humble glory sees himself as no more or less than his fellow man, a characteristic many will strive for and never attain.

~

"What scares me is this world is so unstable with everything; values, respect, and good socialization is being lost in our society. It's easy to push buttons but it is not easy to talk to people. Scary."

How many among us can be tolerant of today's society while seeing without rose-colored glasses that the "old days" are definitely gone? Perhaps a major factor for the average age of motorcycle club members being 35+ is due to the fact that the "old timers" long for the days when families stayed together and defended each other against the negative forces of the world, with the home providing a safe haven for all of us. Clubs are heavily structured and roles are clearly defined. The new world requires each of us to demand respect from our children and teach them to question authority but to also consider one's position before judging their actions. There may well be good reason for a person to act swiftly when we expected the opposite reaction. Z, I believe, would have been happier in an older world for he possesses an old-world charm that this author has only witnessed in the deep, remote countryside of my father's hometown in Italy! Time stands still for men like Z and changing attitudes and sociological advances do not alter his perspective on life and love. His inner strength composes his outer shield, which will never be defeated or dispirited.

Z has always been a leader simply because he is able to see under the surface of an individual. He sees through the facades, searches, and finds the person's valuable qualities and will help uncover those good qualities or even reveal it to the person in possession if they seem blind to their ability.

~

"I feel the people around me contribute in their own way by their abilities. Not everyone is good at everything but when you pool their good abilities it equals success. Together you are a unit."

Z recognizes that a team will always accomplish more than one lone player and using this philosophy he has achieved great success in his life and for his club. Men who are in awe of Z's personable ways would do well to study this man's character. Witness his disposition, his temperament, and his integrity, and eventually the fortitude of the soul is discovered and his reputation is justified. In a recent conflict, Z fell victim to unwarranted criticism and faced that criticism with an unwavering determination to fight for the preservation of his club. He battled the enemy fairly, even though almost impossible, and with the weapons of a strong brotherhood fixed securely behind him. Inevitably, as is always the case, good won against evil, and a mightier legion of Boozefighters members emerged victorious. This result was in large part due to Z's unfaltering convictions and his faith in the loyalty of his brethren.

~

"I had esophageal cancer in 2006 and at the same time Kevlar in my stomach (from a past weight-lifting injury) twisted and was about to cut open my intestine. I have been blessed."

Many people, throughout their lifetime, are forced to endure physical or mental conditions which inevitably spawn some type of mystical revelation and enlightenment. Thus was the case when Z suffered from esophageal cancer in 2006. Most unusual is the way Z learned of his illness, through an Algonquin Medicine Man. While at an Indian powwow, he was introduced to the Medicine Man, Spotted Wolf, who proceeded to tell Z all about his past. He then stated suddenly, "You need to go see a doctor right away." Before Z left him, Spotted Wolf took off his necklace and said, "The Creator has asked me to gift you from my heart my medicine necklace and from my heart I give you my own personal medicine necklace." Twenty minutes later, another Medicine Man from Arizona, named "Man with a Bow," asked Z to sit in a chair. He too told Z about his past, the same information the first man told him, and this one also told him to see a doctor as soon as possible. Z took the wise advice and visited his doctor the next day. His blood tests proved abnormal and after enduring additional medical tests, Z was found to have esophageal cancer, which happened to be in the same spot that Mother Earth (tortoise shell with ivory woman's figure) is depicted on the necklace. The Medicine Man said to Z, "You oversee many and you don't come out of the dark. If needed, you will come out." Z was given his own Indian name, "Shadow Eagle," from Spotted Wolf. Z is convinced that his encounter with the Medicine Men and his quick action (and of course the Medicine Necklace) saved his life.

Dancing so close to death, a man starts to develop a deep appreciation for simple things and will cherish every fleeting moment with his loved ones. This experience strips you of all that is trivial and insignificant, and time suddenly becomes both your best friend and your worst enemy. Beauty and beast collide and it falls on the victim to persevere. A wise woman once said to me, "You can have one hundred people around you night and day but when you're sick, you're sick alone." From these dark days in life a person, whether a survivor or having succumbed to their illness, comes to a certain peace, and that peace surrounds them until the end of their days. Z survived against the odds, bravely facing any obstacles in the path of his good health, and certainly this has contributed to his deep compassion and spiritual awakening. Your spirit travels further when awakened by faith, and every blessing, no matter how small, is counted.

~

"We are not born wise. By not being wise we become wise. To be wise, that comes from experience and conditioning. Age does not change things. There are many who made many mistakes when young and after many years they are still making the same mistakes."

Z has been a strong advocate to me since the day we met, always praising my writing and encouraging me to reach my highest potential. Z has even arranged for me to have unique writing opportunities within the BFMC world and never ceases to remind me that my words, though they may seem to fall on deaf ears at times, do indeed have the potential to change a person's mind or heart. I have sought advice from Z myself many times when I've been unsure of certain club protocol and various issues involving the biker subculture. He guides me in directions which he knows will save me from embarrassment or undue criticism. I am grateful for his trust in me and for keeping me from becoming too jaded and controversial with my thought-process, while at the same time instilling a confidence in me that I never knew I could achieve, especially in a male-dominated subculture. He does promote creativity but has taught me that there must be limits with regard to the biker world. He is a wise, extremely intelligent, judicious, and dedicated club member, as well as a charming man and a wonderful friend to all who know and love him.

~

"I wish I could play a musical instrument and be good at it. Maybe someday."

Perhaps one day Z will allow me to reciprocate by letting me teach him to play the piano. I am truly honored to call Z a friend and am so very glad our flight from Newark that day in October was cancelled. Our chance meeting in the airport changed my life forever. My hopes and dreams for my writing career are even greater now, yet more attainable, because of his support and wise counsel. My guess is that many other men and women have imagined the unlimited possibilities in their lives because of this man called Z.

~

"I can only say one thing.
This is the Greatest Show on Earth"

Z

* I'D RATHER LAUGH WITH THE SINNERS *

~

"I don't know who you are anymore," my mother said to me as we were sipping our coffee at our local coffee shop on a recent Thursday morning. She was lamenting that my main topic of conversation lately is always about bikers. I spent the next half hour trying to convince my mother that I was always like this, she just never noticed until now. Didn't you notice that I never went after "suits" I asked her, or that I always liked the guys who had a wild side? She in fact once dubbed me the "black sheep" of the family, instead of my four mischievous brothers as everyone would assume. What about the simple fact that my wardrobe consists of 90% basic black and my favorite jacket would be my leather. And then there was my introduction to motorcycles, when my cousin Vinny took me for my first ride around the block when I was 15. I never forgot how much I loved it. I remember as a kid, sitting on a Saturday afternoon one day at my family's pizza place, The Pizza Nook, and watching a pack of bikers ride by the restaurant. I went outside to watch them all fly by and secretly wished that *I* was part of that pack. I think about that now whenever I'm riding in a pack and smile to myself realizing that the biker genie must have heard me and continues to grant my wish.

I thought about what it is that makes women like me so attracted to bikers. I can't attribute it to just one thing. I tell my friends that just the sight of a biker's boot on the pedal can turn me on. Is it the "edginess" that these guys seem to have in common, that extra little element of danger that seems to linger around them like an invisible little devil on their shoulder? By the way, bikers always seem to be so damn sexy - the way they walk, the way they talk, the way they dress, that menacing twinkle in their eye, the extra macho-ness that comes naturally to them. Yet there is always a heart – and I love to search and find the hearts of those devils. Many possess an inner strength,

usually the result of some kind of pain, which just adds to their
intensity. I love those desperado types.

Yet, this love of bikers does not limit me from other ventures
in life. I am an excellent secretary, religion teacher, mother of
three, I love to play the piano, enjoy dark, haunting, Broadway
shows like *Phantom of the Opera*, love to crochet and make
baby blankets, and just happen to love hanging out with bikers.
"What a woman!" a male friend of mine recently remarked,
when after rocking out together to a heavy metal tune, I asked
him to listen to a selection from a Puccini opera. He thought
it was cool that I could enjoy both extremes. What can I say, I
love diversity. And I love the excitement I feel when I'm around
bikers. Someone told us, when Dino bought his first bike, that
we were in for the time of our lives. This is so true. I've met so
many good people since we started riding, many who I'm sure
will be lifelong friends.

I love watching bikers when they first meet with each other –
the way all the guys circle the bikes and just stare at them for a
respectful amount of time, commenting on how "sweet" the bike
looks and praising the paint job, etc. I found myself recently
doing the same thing – circling the bike and examining all the
details and what kind of pipes were on the bike. I still can't
identify the kind of bike I'm looking at without verifying it, but
I've definitely learned the difference between a Sportster and a
Road King!

Sometimes when I'm riding on the bike with Dino, my mind
wanders and I start to solve all kinds of little dilemmas in my
head. Riding seems to open my mind to possibilities – maybe it's
being out in the open air, but I will sometimes hop off the bike
with less to worry about then when I hopped on because I have
the problem solved (at least mentally). This is probably one of
the reasons guys love to ride too. Riding is their own brand of
harmony and an excellent way to chase away some shadows.

Then there's the really cool thing that you can take a
motorcycle ride one day, meet about five or ten new people and
be instant friends just by sharing the ride together. Everyone
accepts each other, no questions asked, no judgments, no pre-
requisites to join this club, just the love of riding in common. I
can't think of any other instances in my life where this is true. I
love how I can be friends with male bikers without any romantic

pretense or expectations. Sure, there's always some level of attraction and of course we all love to flirt, but I never feel I have to worry about impressing anyone to get them to like me in this realm. It's an instant camaraderie and it's unique, special, and just plain comfortable.

I know that not every woman gets excited at the sound of a motorcycle in the distance, or turned on by a sea of black T-shirts and bikes, but I also know I am not alone! I am a woman who loves bikers - hear me roar! I will not settle into middle-age repose becoming a couch potato and watching my kids take over the world now that they don't need me as much anymore. My heart now beats louder for the man dressed in black waiting for me to take his hand (and ride to the nearest ice-cream stand)! No more dishes and soap operas to fill my free hours; give me my biker, "Free Bird" in my ears, and a day in the wind – that's my paradise.

So I am once again charmed by the sight of Dino with his bandana and sunglasses on, nodding his head for me to hop on the Harley. My spirit is released as we head out on the bike, passing fields and fragrant flowers along this particular journey, and I laughingly admit to myself that I am enjoying this way too much but if that's a sin, I echo Mr. Billy Joel when he sang, "I'd rather laugh with the sinners than cry with the saints!"

~

* THE GREATEST SHOW ON EARTH *

~

I was lunching recently with some Boozefighters and Z and I were discussing, among other things, the biker subculture in our area. Z said that, taking into account all the characters, the diversity of the people involved with motorcycles, the similarities but huge differences between motorcycle clubs, the conflicts and yes, sometimes drama to be dealt with, he could sum it up in a few words. He said, "Lisa, I say this with great respect for everyone who rides a motorcycle, our culture is the "Greatest Show on Earth." I knew exactly what he meant.

I've met the most interesting people on my journey from biker event to club party to charity rides, to benefits to help a brother's defense, or in honor of a fallen brother. It used to surprise me when I would learn that a biker was also a devoted family man, or that he was a professional businessman in his "other life." Now, nothing surprises me, yet I am continually impressed and amazed with the range of personalities one encounters within the biker culture. I tell my non-biker friends that if our country was run by a biker, we would probably have much less of a problem getting things done. As Carmella has said many times, our elected officials could learn something from watching the respectful behavior of the men at a motorcycle event. This is stuff you should have learned in Kindergarten, yet many outside of this subculture seem to have lost their basic sense of common courtesy or even how to greet each other. For example, at this particular lunch, when I walked into the restaurant, all the men stood up and offered me a chair. It didn't matter that half of them did not expect me to be there; they still accepted my intrusion and greeted me with open arms. This happens whenever I'm around bikers, not just my favorite Boozefighters.

Maybe it's because bikers are in a way forced to learn to respect each other, and I'm not just referring to prospects of motorcycle clubs, I mean respect from the road to the bar. If at first that seems unfair (the notion that you "earn" respect), it really is a lesson everyone should study. Of course there are those men who grew up in the kind of household where the women were adored and treated like princesses (my house was like that, lucky me, the only girl with four brothers and a strict Italian father), and I find those men already seem to know the respect "ropes," but we are not all that fortunate to have been guided by respectful role models. This is where the wise old greybeard enters the picture. He is the one who passes on the traditions and the values that bikers hold in high esteem. It is a combination of those traditions and values which serve as the beacons in times of conflict. Those who honor such principles are the ones who survive and thrive for future generations. I've seen the conflicts, I've seen some drama, and I have witnessed bravery, determination, and courage against some pretty big odds. For these and many other personal reasons, I am so very proud to know and love the New York riders in this "Greatest Show on Earth."

~

* ANSWERS *

~

Since I asked all the participants in this book to answer questions, I felt it was only fair that I do the same. Here, then, are *my* answers:

My most defining moment was the birth of my first child. Suddenly I knew that everything that happened to me up to that point in my life was now insignificant, that my child was now the most, and maybe the *only*, important person in my life. I was honored to call myself a mother and I felt that way with the birth of each of my children.

I grew up in a very traditional Italian family with four brothers, Frank, the oldest, Tony, a year younger than me, Marco, and Rocco. My father was born in Italy and moved to the United States in his early 20's, met and married my mother, also 100% Italian, then settled in Albany, New York. My father taught us to be very proud of our heritage. Our family dinners always included wine at the table and lots of pasta and homemade Italian bread. My parents celebrated their 50th wedding anniversary in 2007. My brothers and I are close, we see each other often, and we all live near our parents.

In addition to working for a major power company, my father owned and operated a pizza restaurant called the Pizza Nook. A vivid memory of mine is hanging out at the Pizza Nook on Saturday afternoons while my mother was working. One Saturday every summer, there would be a huge pack of bikers passing by the shop. I would run outside when I heard them coming so that I could watch them ride by, jealously waving as I stood there. I would think to myself, "I wish I could be a part of that someday." I loved seeing all the leather and the smiles on the faces of the women on the back of the bikes. I knew I'd be smiling too if that was me! Sometimes I think that was the beginning of my "attraction" to bikers. Years later, when I rode in a pack for the first time, I felt as if a long-awaited dream had finally come true.

My first time on a motorcycle was when I was about 15 years old and my cousin Vinny asked me if I'd like to take a little ride with him. I hopped on the bike and even though we only rode around the block, I can still remember how much I *loved* it. It was so thrilling to me and I thought to myself, I definitely have to do that again! There were no other opportunities, however, until Dino bought a bike in 1998. We waited till our girls were older before we started riding together. Then, in 2001, our son was born so I had to take another hiatus from the bike and focus on diapers and car seats again.

When I became involved with *New York Rider Magazine* in 2005, Dino and I started riding a lot more and we haven't stopped yet. I have recently enrolled in the Motorcycle Safety Foundation course to pursue my own motorcycle license.

I have been working for the State Education Department as a Secretary for 30 years, although I've been part-time since my first child was born in 1989. I have been the Editor of *New York Rider Magazine* since 2007. I have also been a Catechist for ten years at Christ Our Light Catholic Church. Ironically, my experience teaching the children has complimented my experience interviewing bikers. This could be because the personalities are so diverse and I've had to learn all about individual learning styles in order to interact on their level, similarly educating myself on the biker culture (outlaws, weekend warriors, etc.) Perhaps it has more to do with the fact that children and bikers share a natural sense of freedom and excitement. Regardless of the reasons, both generations have helped me with my own personal insecurities and enhanced my skills at teaching and interviewing.

I regret not traveling more when I was younger. I have some wonderful memories of my trips to Europe with my father and later with my best friend, Nancy. I also regret not concentrating more on the study of piano. The piano is a very strong passion of mine and I feel I might have enjoyed a musical career if I had started earlier in life. For now, I am content with practicing my intermediate sheet music, particularly classical pieces.

I would like to go back to Rome, Italy someday and revisit St. Peter's Basilica since I didn't pay enough attention the first time, and hope to someday see an opera with my father, at the Metropolitan Opera House in New York City.

~

"Let your soul take you where you long to be"
(Phantom of the Opera)

* THREAT ASSESSMENT OF BIKER CLUBS: A CONFLICT OF SOCIAL IDENTITY FOR GOVERNMENT AGENCIES *

(By Professor Eric R. Carlson, MS CAS)

In perusing the recently released National Gang Assessment Report of 2011 by the Federal Bureau of Investigation, I immediately noticed the publication's attempt to offer an operational definition of what defines a gang. However, what was actually portrayed was a muddled and broad definition linking biker clubs and gangs together as though they are synonymous.

Interestingly, the report identifies several legally sanctioned "American Biker" motorcycle clubs as fitting the gang definition by referring to them as "outlaw motorcycle gangs." The publication seems to strategically utilize the classic "guilt by association" method in developing a threat determination. By associating "gangs," who are purely and intentionally a criminal enterprise, to legitimate motorcycle clubs, the government presents a false aura of threat. Oddly, the report, although it does not cite what types of objective data were utilized in determining the level of "OMG" threat, actually displays in graphs and charts the OMG's as a VERY LOW LEVEL of threat compared with all other gang/ groups depicted therein.

Hence, motorcycle clubs should not be included in the extensive report as a threat to society or the community nor should they be webbed into the extremely dangerous gang-style activity actually committed by gangs in the United States. Gang lifestyle and the American Biker Culture are two completely different planets in comparison. Despite their own statistical measures, law enforcement and governmental agencies seem to consistently support and promote the discriminatory stereotype that motorcycle clubs such as the Hells Angels are not clubs at all but are dangerous criminal enterprises that pose significant threat to the health and well-being of civilized communities. Interestingly enough, these aforementioned communities seem to disagree. Recent community surveys indicate two thirds of individuals (over 65%) consistently report that they do not perceive bikers or biker clubs as a threat and the percentage that do is not a statistically significant percentage.

Why, then, is law enforcement so passionately selling to the public this false set of beliefs? What are the psychological underpinnings that drive these false notions which are used to justify unnecessary enforcement tactics against bikers and the biker culture as well as in the misuse of resources that would be better spent on fighting real threats? When no real community threat exists, why do government agencies construct one?

The answer may lie in fairly basic principles of social psychology. One takes the inaccurate stereotyping of the perceived "out group" {bikers} in order to maintain the "in group" {police} and this is achieved through controlled definition of social identities or social standing/status. The media, used by agencies to propagate the social stigma, creates a schema in which we are supposed to organize our thinking and perceptions about bikers and the biker culture. The foundation of that schema derives from other media sources of information like the movie, "The Wild Ones", starring Marlon Brando and Lee Marvin, which portray all bikers as angry, rebellious fringe members of society looking for trouble through criminal opportunity. This misinformation campaign aids in strengthening the government's stereotyping of bikers and oddly legitimizes the threat assessment on biker clubs, in general.

Yet, the facts do not support the use of this broad brush discrimination against the American Biker Culture. The facts DO support the American Biker Culture as a diverse group of Americans who possess a clear independent streak in nature, quite like our forefathers, and many of whom have defended this country and are veterans. Independence is not wholly criminal; in fact many would argue it is quite patriotic. The rub or conflict is clear that the social identity of police groups derive and function from the premise that they are the marshals in town, the sole enforcers of their "correct brand of justice" dictated to them by the powers that be. All citizens must first respect the patch and colors representing the government in power and most importantly fall back in fear and in servitude. Those in the American Biker Culture are not the fall-back types who adhere to coercion, force or unjust intrusions on their exercise for liberty and freedom.

In conclusion, it is quite apparent from the content of the report herein noted, my research, and professional experience (I, personally, do not know any bikers or any members of biker clubs) that the actual threat created by the existence of motorcycle clubs and the biker culture IS NOT one suffered by our communities, but rather a serious threat to the social identity of groups within our society such as police and governmental agencies who hold power and authority above the citizen but whose misuse of authority has repeatedly come under continued scrutiny. Such agencies must, as a matter of survival, justify their behavior and decisions which many times threaten the life and liberty of citizens and do so by means of profiling, unjust stereotyping and even falsely accusing groups and cultures within society that they determine is a threat to the government, first and foremost.

{Eric R. Carlson is a Professor of Psychology at Schenectady County Community College and the State University of New York at Albany}

~

* LISA'S PEACE *
~

I have fulfilled all of the dreams I had when I was younger and thought about where I wanted to be when I "grew up." Getting married, having children, owning a home, seeing my parents grow old together and enjoying their grandchildren were all the things I hoped I would have, and I have been blessed with each.

I never expected to receive one of my greatest gifts at this time in my life – the gift of a whole circle of friends from the biker world. I cannot express what the last few years has meant to me, having met some of the most interesting, intelligent, wise, *wild,* and certainly unforgettable, people to cross my path. The stories that some have shared with me have touched my heart and have carried my soul to even greater depths of compassion. The relationships I've been fortunate to have accepted into my life have taught me more about what it means to love a friend, and to feel that love reciprocated with every meeting. Anyone who might think I am a good writer needs to know that my writing is only as good as my inspiration. My inspiration comes from the people around me, my family members, and my "biker" friends who seem to realize more than most the value of each day, and the importance of cherishing and loving every moment we spend together.

My rewards for writing about bikers are much more valuable than any financial compensation I could ever receive. Anyone who is involved in the motorcycle community knows that the friends you acquire through biker events are too numerous to count. However, I can safely say my world has expanded ten-fold since working for *New York Rider Magazine.* I have met literally *hundreds* of people and many of them are now more than just friends or acquaintances.

I have made connections with other writers and have enjoyed honing my own writing skills in the process. Interviewing people is something I had no experience with, and there is always room for improvement, but through the process of developing questions and talking to people in the motorcycle industry, I have shed a lot of the self-consciousness I used to have when approaching someone for the first time. It has now become almost second-nature for me to be just a little more inquisitive every time I meet a new bike builder or members of a new motorcycle or riding club. As a result of my writing, I am recognized by many people in the biker community and treated with respect, another priceless gift, in my opinion. One of the proudest days of my life was the day the Hells Angels of Troy, New York, presented both Carmella and I each with a gold necklace, the words "81 Supports You" on the pendant, as a token of their appreciation for our work on their behalf with *New York Rider Magazine*. The ultimate reward comes when someone tells me they love my work and read every word. To a writer, those sentiments are very much appreciated and cherished. I am proud to have a "voice" in my local motorcycle community, and grateful to the men and women who have allowed me to represent them in my articles.

I treasure my family and all the bikers I have met, near and far, the ones I see often, and the ones I see only once or twice a year, who have changed my life and continue to inspire me every day.

Lisa Petrocelli & Carmella Brown

* WORDS *

~

~ Ambitious, Powerful, Conviction, Old-School, Fierce, Photographer, Turbulent, Pride, Courage, Righteous, Faith, Confidence, Intimidating, Survivor, Wisdom ~

If you have read this far, hopefully you can see that the words used to describe each man apply to all of them. One of the principles of a motorcycle club is that each member has their own strengths to "bring to the table." Although not everyone in this book is a club member, that same principle is found when comparing the characteristics of these men. I chose to focus on the dominant characteristic of each individual.

One may argue that we would find similar traits in any specific group of people, and that is true. However, something sets bikers apart from any other culture. They all have a certain restlessness about them, most are bold and maybe more defiant when provoked. Bikers never run from a fight and they usually prefer to resolve their own conflicts. They believe that justice should be served by their own means/actions. Bikers are more direct, prefer to tackle issues head-on, and are not as judgmental as the majority of the population can be. These guys may appear to be "bad boys" or rebellious renegades, when in fact they all have a sense of gallantry about them. They really are a different animal in the kingdom. Incidentally, these chapters reflect each man's character during the period of time I have known them. I have learned from the biker subculture that everyone is responsible for maintaining their character, their principles and their honor.

I cannot deny the evidence of criminal behavior in some motorcycle clubs, but an unfortunate consequence of those incidences is that many bikers are categorized in the same way – as criminals or the outlaws of society who don't care about anyone but themselves. This generalization has caused a stigma that may never be erased, but we will continue to try to counter the effects of the "bad apples" so they don't spoil the whole bunch.

My intentions for this book were to present these people to my readers and somehow memorialize each of them as a token of my appreciation for their friendship and what they have brought to my life. These men have altered my own perception and misconceptions about bikers and for that I am grateful. The essays included in between chapters were written to document my experiences in the biker community. I hope I have begun to open your own mind to the prejudice you may be holding against bikers or any other subculture that may be different from your own.

If anyone reading this is more inclined to lift their own veil of prejudice, then I will have realized my dream. Peace +

* ACKNOWLEDGMENTS *

~

I thank the following people for helping to make this book a reality:

➢ First, thank you to my husband, Dino, for letting me be me and for encouraging the pursuit of my passions. I love you.

➢ Thank you to our parents for taking such good care of our children while Dino and I went out to "play with the bikers."

➢ Special thanks to Hank McGrath, my brother, Rocco Padula, and my son, Dino Jr., for helping with editing!

➢ Thanks to Lee Sikes of Broadway Choppers for the motorcycle parts used in the cover photo.

➢ Thanks to the Boozefighters Motorcycle Club for their unceasing love and support. You are my brothers.

➢ Special thanks to Z of the Boozefighters Mountain Chapter 60, for his advice, support, and encouragement from the beginning to the end of this project.

➢ Thank you to Hank McGrath, who has been a wonderful friend and advisor. His support and collaboration with me on this book has been invaluable.

➢ Thanks to all the men in this book for trusting me with their stories, and to ALL the motorcycle clubs in my neck of the woods that have accepted me into their world and respected my work.

➢ Special thanks to Carmella Brown, owner of *New York Rider Magazine,* for bringing me deeper into the world of bikers, for allowing me to be as creative as possible with my writing for the magazine, and especially for being my precious friend.

New York Rider Magazine has played a major part in any success I achieve as a writer. I love you Carmella!

➢ Finally, thank you to my children, Sara, Sophia, and Dino Jr., for all the strength and love I will ever need. You are my inspiration.

~

Index